IMPLEMENT
or DIE

Mike Shorten

Getting your strategy to work for you

A book to help you run a more successful organization by defining and implementing strategies

Simplify
TOM

I0063532

First published by Mike Shorten, 2022

Copyright © 2022 by Mike Shorten

ISBN-978-0-620-95296-5 (print)

ISBN-978-0-620-95297-2 (eBook)

Title: Implement or Die

Publisher: SimplifyTOM (Pty) Ltd

(www.simplifytom.com)

Editor: Phillipa Mitchell

(www.phillipamitchell.com)

Proofreader: Ricky Woods

(rickywoods604@gmail.com)

Cover design and layout by Gregg Davies Media

(greggdavies.com)

All rights reserved.

The moral right of the author has been asserted.

No part of this publication may be reproduced, distributed, or transmitted in any form or by any means, including photocopying, recording, or other electronic or mechanical methods, without the prior written permission of the author, except in the case of brief quotations embodied in critical reviews and certain other non-commercial uses permitted by copyright law.

Additional copies of this book can be purchased from all leading book retailers worldwide.

Disclaimer

The writer and publisher have made every attempt to ensure the accuracy and reliability of the information provided in this tool. However, the information is provided "as is" without warranty of any kind. The writer and publisher do not accept any responsibility or liability for the accuracy, content, completeness, legality, or reliability of the information contained in this tool.

No warranties, promises and/or representations of any kind, expressed or implied, are given as to the nature, standard, accuracy or otherwise of the information provided in this tool nor to the suitability or otherwise of the information to your particular circumstances.

We shall not be liable for any loss or damage of whatever nature (direct, indirect, consequential, or other) whether arising in contract, tort or otherwise, which may occur as a result of your use of (or inability to use) this tool, or from your use of (or failure to use) the information in this tool.

Any reliance you place on this tool is therefore strictly at your own risk.

This tool provides references to other information and material owned by third parties. The additional or other content of these third parties is not within our control, and we cannot and will not take responsibility for the information or content thereof. Reference to such third parties is not taken as an endorsement of the third parties, or any products promoted, offered or sold by the third party.

Contents

Why I Wrote This Book

The rate of new business failure is high:[1]

20%	30%	50%
The number of businesses that will fail in the first year	The number of businesses that will fail by Year 2	The number of businesses that will fail by Year 5

There is, coincidently, a high failure rate among organizations that fail to implement their strategies:[2]

67% of organizational strategies are never fully implemented

---

1   U.S. Bureau of Labor Statistics, 2016, Survival Rates of Establishments, by year started and number of years since starting, 1994–2015, in percent, <https://www.bls.gov/bdm/entrepreneurship/bdm_chart3.htm>.

2   Ron Carucci, 2017, Executives Fail to Execute Strategy Because They're Too Internally Focused, Harvard Business Review, <https://hbr.org/2017/11/executives-fail-to-execute-strategy-because-they-re-too-internally-focused>.

Conversely, organizations that successfully implement their strategies realize financial gains:[3]

77% of organizations that successfully implement their strategy, realize successful financial outcomes

These statistics show that organizations need to define appropriate strategies at a level that enables their implementation to be successful. That's easy to say but difficult to do! I felt I needed to do something to help organizations with their strategy implementation success rates.

I have spent a fair portion of my career with one of the world's large international consulting firms, helping organizations define their strategies and develop plans to improve their business performance. Acutely aware of the cost and effectiveness of advisory services, I felt I needed to consolidate my knowledge and experience into a tool aimed at strategy definition and implementation. I wanted a cost-effective way of getting this knowledge to organizations that could not afford consultants.

The most cost-effective method, I felt, was through a book. There are many books out there espousing many different managerial theories or pushing academic agendas, but I wanted to write one that focused on covering key concepts that organizations needed to get right, without the need to pass the "thud test" (that being the sound made by a large book hitting the table). I also wanted to leave the responsibility for design and implementation where it should be – with the organization's leadership.

---

3   Gary L. Neilson, Karla L. Martin, and Elizabeth Powers, 2008, The Secrets to Successful Strategy Execution, Harvard Business Review, <https://hbr.org/2008/06/the-secrets-to-successful-strategy-execution>.

To do all of this, I needed to simplify. I firmly believe that complexity and failure work hand in hand, and thus wanted to see a simplified approach to providing advice that would hopefully lead to a simplification of solutions by the user.

This book defines a **business improvement** and **strategy implementation** tool designed to help organizations realize business success through identifying and implementing strategies and tactics to achieve their vision. The tool provides a simplified, holistic, and action-oriented approach to achieving success, no matter the kind of organization.

The Tool and How to Use it

This book is presented as a business tool that has been designed to help organizations to be successful by providing a comprehensive but simplified approach to improving their performance while striving to achieve a future vision.

The tool starts with a vision for the organization's future and a strategy that defines how the vision will be attained. Strategies are, by nature, high-level and often lack the detail required to automatically ensure successful implementation. More detail is required as to what needs to change at the operating model level. (The operating model refers to how products and services are delivered to meet customer needs). To help define the required changes, a future operating model needs to be determined – also known as a Target Operating Model (or TOM). The TOM covers all aspects of the organization, including markets, operations, and people. A detailed implementation plan then helps the organization bridge the gap from how they currently operate to how they want to operate to ensure delivery of their vision and strategy. This tool helps you define this necessary detail by reviewing your current practices against best practices. It also alerts you to the numerous pitfalls in strategy implementation that you need to avoid to attain your vision.

AN OVERVIEW

Despite all its mystique and the confusion that surrounds it, a strategy is actually quite simple. It highlights who an organization is (or wants to be), what it does (or wants to do), and provides an essential growth path for the organization to follow to achieve its envisaged future. The tool builds on these three essential elements as shown in the diagram below:

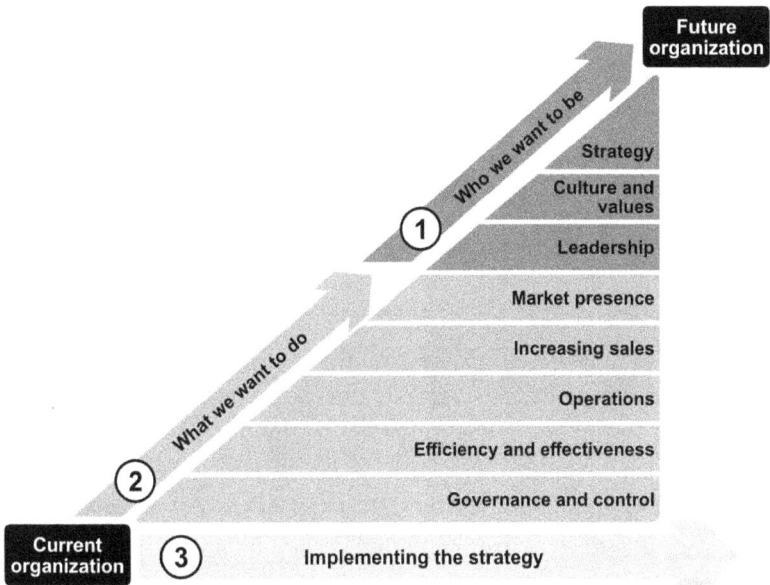

An Overview of the Tool

The first step in the process is defining **who the organization wants to be** ①. This involves defining the strategy (purpose, vision, mission, goals, and objectives), the culture and values (since people are critical in achieving the vision), and the leadership style necessary to achieve the vision.

The second step is deciding **what the organization wants to do** ② in order to become what it wants to be. This is achieved by defining market presence, increasing sales, operations and delivery, efficiency and effectiveness, and governance and control.

The final step is ensuring that **the strategies are implemented** ③.

Each element in the triangle in the above model is represented by a **module** in the tool. Each module is supported by a number of **key management strategies**. The management strategies go into extensive detail on each topic, providing additional information such as actions, tools, examples, and best practices to help you with your detailed definition.

USING THE TOOL

Running a business is complex. The tool has many different facets catering to many of these complexities. So, where do you start?

The order of the tool is very specific, starting with the modules that will help you define **who the organization wants to be**. The next modules will provide guidance to defining **what the organization wants to do**. The final section is about ensuring success in implementing your strategies, as identified in the previous modules.

Each managerial strategy starts with a brief description of the topic aimed at creating **awareness**. Next, **actions** are provided to help draw up plans and begin changing your organization through implementation. You might want to undertake further research on the topic before committing to any actions, which is perfectly acceptable – it is your intervention in your organization. Do what you feel is best.

You can read through the entire tool in less than a day. But to reflect fully on each action and its implications for your organization, and to formulate and implement solutions, will take much longer. You can use the tool continuously, independent of your strategy definition process. Organizations are dynamic. You will get something new each time you go through the tool.

As a final note, do not expect to find all the answers to your organization's issues to be neatly laid out in the tool. Using the tool is only the beginning of your journey. I hope to widen your knowledge and stimulate your thinking. You are still going to have to work out how to use the different concepts in your organization and then make them work through implementation.

The biggest challenge facing you in using this tool is overcoming all your other priorities and challenges and sticking to implementing your strategy. There are going to be all sorts of immediate demands on your time, taking you away from implementing solutions for your long-term growth. You are going to find the going hard, and you will, at times, ask yourself why you are doing this.

Keep the end picture of your organization in mind. This won't happen overnight. Your reward will be a successful organization that will keep you excited while it is developing into your envisaged future organization.

You might want to find a mentor with who you can discuss your progress in implementing your strategy. That person will be your counselor, consultant, and cheerleader.

WHO WE WANT THE ORGANIZATION TO BE

This is the first section outlined in the approach and covers **who we want the organization to be**. It is highlighted in the diagram below:

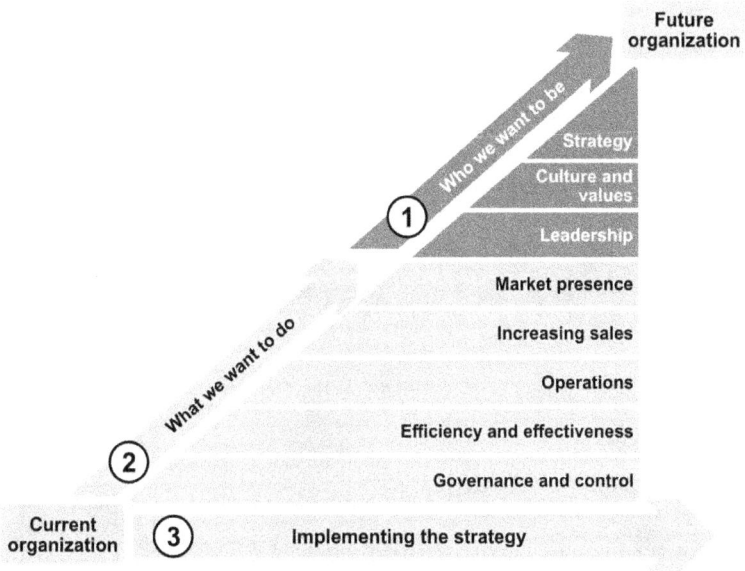

Section 1 of the Tool

The details of this section are shown in the model below:

Module Content

The Strategy Module

The tool starts with defining *where you are going*. This includes the definition of purpose, vision, and mission statements answering the why, what, and how questions.

Once an overall strategy is defined, *measurements of success* are determined through goals and objectives. *Getting there* is defined through strategies and tactics to help you achieve your strategy.

The Culture and Values Module

Your culture will ultimately determine the type of organization you will have and how successful you will be. A key component of your culture is your values. You cannot deliver your vision without the commitment of the people who will be involved in making the vision happen – your employees. Great vision, mission, and purpose statements resonate with employees when they address what already exists in their hearts and minds. Implementing these requires active management of any change.

The Leading the Team Module

Do you have the right leadership team to attain your vision? This module covers leadership and delegation, teamwork, your influence on the organization, and your support network.

The Reviewing Your Strategy Module

This module allows you to reflect on your strategy.

Your definitions resulting from these modules become the driving framework for the definition of your Target Operating Model as detailed in the next section.

1

Strategy

Your strategy is your organization's high-level work plan defining where you are going and how you are going to get there.

Your strategy:

- Helps clarify your thinking by providing a systematic approach that will help you define what you want for your organization and how you are going to achieve it.

- Will help redirect your focus should the organization lose its way.

- Provides an opportunity to explore ideas for the future and to share and discuss opportunities and ideas clearly and consistently.

- Provides a common purpose that tells employees what you are trying to do.

- Helps generate hope and enthusiasm for the future, both for yourself and for your employees.

- Helps provide focus and direction, particularly when it comes to decision-making and especially when deciding where to allocate scarce resources.

- Provides an overview of the organization, particularly for investors, financiers, and directors, but also for suppliers and even for customers.

The result of a clearly defined and implemented strategy is a sustainable organization.

A typical strategy definition process is depicted in the diagram below:

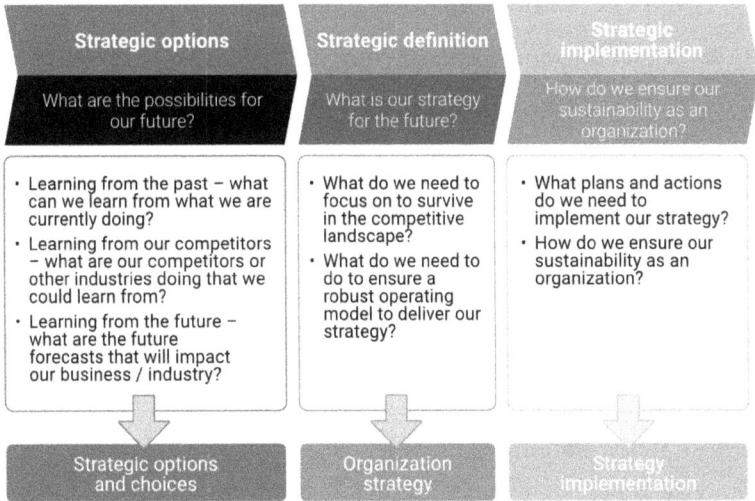

Strategic options	Strategic definition	Strategic implementation
What are the possibilities for our future?	What is our strategy for the future?	How do we ensure our sustainability as an organization?
• Learning from the past – what can we learn from what we are currently doing? • Learning from our competitors – what are our competitors or other industries doing that we could learn from? • Learning from the future – what are the future forecasts that will impact our business / industry?	• What do we need to focus on to survive in the competitive landscape? • What do we need to do to ensure a robust operating model to deliver our strategy?	• What plans and actions do we need to implement our strategy? • How do we ensure our sustainability as an organization?
Strategic options and choices	Organization strategy	Strategy implementation

This module assumes that you have already defined your strategic options and focuses on your strategic definition.

Success and reputation are driven by a few key attributes that need to be considered during your strategy definition process, including:

- Emotional appeal: the organization is trusted, admired, and respected.

- Products and services: products and services are innovative, of high quality, and good value.

- Vision and leadership: the organization has a clear vision of its future. It has excellent leadership that takes advantage of opportunities.

- Workplace: the organization is well managed and is an attractive place at which to work.

- Performance: the organization has a good profit history, shows continued growth, and outperforms its competitors.

- Social responsibility: the organization treats its people well, is environmentally responsible and supports worthwhile causes.

Defining a strategy is not difficult. It is more than likely that you already know and understand all the elements that will make up your strategy. However, the process is not always plain sailing and can lead to procrastination, frustration, and conflict owing to differences in opinion.

A strategy statement must be clear and in writing. A verbal strategy tends to change depending on the audience and the thoughts going through the mind of the CEO or owner at the time! This leads to confusion and, ultimately, to employee dissatisfaction and poor performance. A formal written document provides clarity and consistency to others and helps them to understand what you are trying to achieve. (See *GUIDELINES FOR A GOOD STRATEGY*)

How do you make your strategy live? You are going to aim at referring to your strategy daily to ensure its successful implementation through summarizing your strategy on one page. One page keeps it simple and focused, makes it an effective communication tool, and makes it easier to refer to consistently. The contents of a one-page strategy are up to you. It could just be your purpose, vision, and mission. You can also include your goals, objectives, and core strategies. What about your values? Make your one-page strategy relevant to your needs.

Supporting this one-page strategy statement will be the details of your strategy and implementation plan necessary for its successful implementation.

GUIDELINES FOR A GOOD STRATEGY

- Simplicity: Aim at making a potentially complex subject simple.
- Focus: Clarify what is essential to run and grow the organization successfully.
- Readily understandable: Clearly address all major issues applicable to all stakeholders.
- Versatility: It must be a tool that can be used to communicate with multiple audiences.
- Consistency: Make sure its message is consistent throughout.
- Flexibility: It must be easy to change, update and expand.

1.1 Your Purpose (Why)

The first step in defining your strategy focusses on where you are going and includes your purpose, vison and mission.

AWARENESS

Simon Sinek, in his book *Start With Why*[4], contends that organizations that stand out from their competitors are those that know why they exist. He discovered what he calls "The Golden Circle", which comprises:

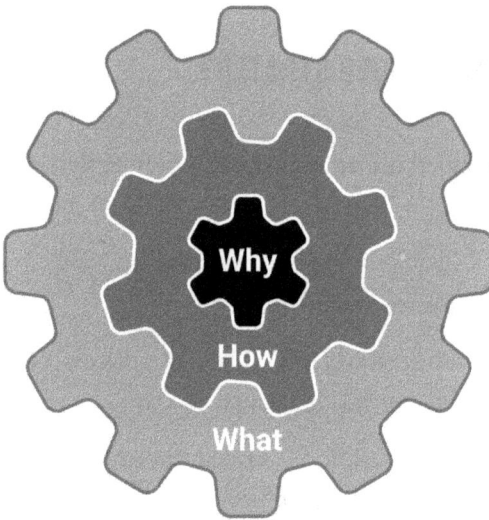

Sinek's Golden Circle

What

Every organization knows WHAT they do. Everyone can describe their products and services.

---

4   Simon Sinek, Start With Why, Penguin Random House, 2011.

How

Not all organizations know HOW they do what they do. HOWs – also known as "differentiating value propositions" or "unique selling propositions" – explain how something is different or better.

Why

Very few organizations can articulate WHY they do what they do. It is not about having a successful organization – that is the result. The WHY is your purpose – what you believe in. WHY does your organization exist?

Sinek quotes Apple as an organization that knows its WHY. Apple's WHY is to challenge the status quo and to empower the individual. Technically, Apple is no different from its competitors. However, they have been enormously successful in areas that are not directly related to their initial service offering (i.e. personal computers). This is something their competitors have not been as successful at doing. Sinek puts this down to Apple knowing their WHY.

Some companies, like Walmart, have at some stage forgotten their WHY. When Sam Walton started Walmart, his WHY was to help people and communities by providing products at a low cost. After his death, however, the company focused solely on low prices. It became a cut-throat business toward its suppliers, employees, and communities and got itself into serious trouble as a result.

We need to understand WHY we exist. WHY is the reason customers buy from us. The HOW and the WHAT follow the WHY. What makes defining your WHY difficult is that customers will usually ask for your HOW and your WHAT but will rarely ask for your WHY.

Once you know your WHY, the challenge lies in staying true to it.

There is often confusion between the vision, mission, and purpose of an organization, with many different definitions for each of these terms. To make things clearer, I have decided to link each of these strategy elements to Sinek's three questions.

- Vision statement: a statement of WHAT a successful future looks like for the organization and where it is headed. A vision statement is aspirational and inspirational.
- Mission statement: a statement of HOW the vision will be achieved? HOW are you going to win?
- Purpose statement: a statement of WHY the organization exists.

But why is a purpose statement necessary?

- Customers prefer to do business with socially conscious organizations.
- The best job applicants seek to be employed by companies with strong ethics and values.
- Employee morale is substantially higher in organizations that are involved in their communities.
- Employees are more productive, more motivated, work harder, and are more creative in organizations whose values align with their personal values.

A good purpose statement can help you attract more customers and harder-working employees.

Example:

The business is an industrial kitchen that has no space for patrons or takeaways. They deliver restaurant-quality meals directly to people in their homes. Their *What, How,* and *Why* can be defined as:

- *What (Vision):* Serving restaurant-quality meals in every home
- *How (Mission):* We create and distribute great-tasting, healthy, organic meals.
- *Why (Purpose):* You can eat healthy, great quality, pre-prepared food in your home.

ACTION

The following actions will help you to define your organization's purpose statement:

- Trace your origins from when you started your organization to where you are today. Why did you start the organization? What problem are you solving? What opportunity are you taking advantage of? What are the highlights of your journey? What values do you uphold?

- What impact has your organization made? What benefits have customers experienced as a result of your organization? What impact has your organization had on employees? What impact has your organization had on local communities? What would happen to these people should your organization cease to exist?

- Review your origins and impacts and ask *why*? (See *EXAMPLES OF WHYs*)

- Craft your purpose. Involve your employees in its definition. Again ask, *Why.*

- Write down your *Why.*

- Publish your *Why.* Use it to attract customers and employees and to guide your organization.

- Update your one-page strategy statement.

EXAMPLES OF WHYs

Simon Sinek's *Why* is: "We imagine a world in which the vast majority of people wake up inspired, feel safe wherever they are, and end the day fulfilled by the work they do."

Below are several successful organizations that have clearly defined *Whys*:[5]

Asana is a teamwork communication manager that provides workspaces, projects, deadlines, and comments that update in real time without the use of emails. Their *Why* is that it sucks to waste unnecessary time trying to communicate instead of getting work done.

Uber has made waves throughout the world with its disruptive approach to ride-sharing services. Their *Why* is that it sucks to be stranded without easy access to reliable transportation.

Bellroy makes leather wallets. Their *Why* is that a fat wallet is literally a pain in the butt.

GoldieBlox creates engineering tools toys for girls to help correct the gender imbalance in engineering. Their *Why* is that girls are discouraged from building things, and they need to change that.

Airbnb's *Why* is that traveling could and should be so much more intimate than staying at hotels.

PK Clean converts plastic waste into reusable oil. Their *Why* is that the future cannot be a giant landfill.

---

5   Samuel Hum, 2021, Start With Why: Mission Statements Simon Sinek Would Approve, Referral Candy, https://www.referralcandy.com/blog/start-with-why-examples/>.

Ministry of Supply makes next-generation performance professional attire. Their *Why* is that office wear shouldn't have to be uncomfortable.

Warby Parker designs and sells affordable and stylish eyewear in its online store. Their *Why* is that stylish eyewear shouldn't have to cost an arm and leg.

1.2 Your Vision (What)

AWARENESS

Great journeys start with a vision. The vision is the dream. It states WHAT you want and where you would like the organization to be in three to five years (or any time period relevant to your organization).

The vision spells out the future state of your organization. It should create passion, be inspirational, be easy to read, paint a realistic picture of the future, stimulate thinking, and demand stretch. The stretch in your vision helps define your aspirations for your organization. It is there to force the organization to think differently and keep ahead of its competitors. The stretch is there to take you out of your comfort zone – to have a vision for your organization that goes beyond your current expectations. The extent of your stretch depends on your current situation, and your people, and often requires strong and visionary leadership to be successful.

Don't be restricted by current performance or issues when defining where you want to be. If your vision is important enough, you will find ways to achieve it. The limiting factors to an organization's growth are not necessarily funds, time, resources, or people. The limiting factor is often its vision. At this stage, you don't have to know how you will achieve your vision. All you need is the belief that you can achieve it. It's amazing what you can accomplish once everyone gets behind attaining the vision.

As you get closer to achieving your vision, you are less likely to have the continued energy to move beyond it. Accordingly, the vision needs to be reinvented as you grow closer to achieving it.

It is the responsibility of the CEO or owner to define a vision and communicate it to employees.

Example:

Think back to the industrial kitchen restaurant that delivers restaurant-quality meals directly to people in their homes. A possible vision for the business is "Serving restaurant-quality meals in every home."

ACTION

The following actions will help you to define your organization's vision:

- Determine the organization you want. (See *WHAT ORGANIZATION DO YOU WANT?*)
- Define an aspirational "stretch vision" for the organization and discuss it with your top management team. (See *DEFINING A VISION* and *EXAMPLES OF VISION STATEMENTS*)
- Continually (daily) find opportunities to share your vision of the future with your employees. Make sure they

understand what you are trying to achieve and know their role in achieving the vision. Get feedback on what they think of the vision and their part in achieving it.

- Inspire your management team to "live" the vision in all their daily dealings.

- Share your vision with the organization's stakeholders, including customers, suppliers, investors, and financiers. You may be surprised at the extent to which they will want to help you.

- When you have a significant decision to make, go back to your vision and make sure you align your decision to the vision.

- Update your one-page strategy statement.

WHAT ORGANIZATION DO YOU WANT?

Begin by doing some brainstorming and answer the following questions when defining the organization you want. The questions are futuristic because you are defining the organization you want, not necessarily the organization you have. In answering each question, start with a long list of descriptive words or phrases and narrow them down to the three that most aptly describe the kind of organization you want.

- Describe your customers by category. Who will you be serving, and who *will you not* be serving?

- What value will you deliver to your customers in the future? Bear in mind their changing needs.

- What new competencies (a combination of skills and technologies) do you need to develop to deliver this value?

- What are the implications of how you interact with your customers (new customer groups, new channels, new priorities)?

- What products or services (or combination thereof) will you offer? What characteristics make them unique? What will your products or services *not* do?

- What is your desired reputation for your organization?

- What targets are you setting for the organization, and by when do you want to achieve them?

- What people, facilities, and systems do you need in place (and by when) if you are to make the future organization operational?

- Who do you intend to partner with? What strategic alliances do you require?

- How do you want to interact with your employees, suppliers, and customers?

- Where will your organization operate?

- Who can provide professional and strategic advice that will help you to grow your organization?

- How will this organization be financed? What will convince investors to invest in or banks to loan money to your organization?

- What will your role be as owner or CEO? How will you spend your time?

- How will your personal beliefs impact this organization?

- Do some research. Look at the visions of companies or organizations you admire. What do you like about their visions?

Don't discard all the ideas you have captured. You will refer back to them throughout this strategy process as well as when implementing other modules.

DEFINING A VISION

Once you have defined the organization you want, define a first draft vision. A vision should be a picture of your organization in the future. Your vision should be an inspiration to you and your employees. It is an opportunity to articulate your dreams and hopes and should be audacious with an element of "stretch". Aim at being wildly optimistic with no limits – it is a "picture" of the future but not the means to get there.

Your vision should become a guide for all your strategic planning.

Typically, a vision could include:

- A time period and targets.
- The type of organization you are and where you will be positioned in the market.
- Something about your products or services.
- Who you want to work with.
- What you want your customers to know you for.
- The work experience you want for your employees.

EXAMPLES OF VISION STATEMENTS

Examples of leading vision statements include:[6]

Alzheimer's Association: A world without Alzheimer's disease.

---

6   Lindsay Kolowich Cox, 27 Truly Inspiring Company Vision and Mission Statement Examples, Hub-Spot, <https://blog.hubspot.com/marketing/inspiring-company-mission-statements>.

Teach for America: One day, all children in this nation will have the opportunity to attain an excellent education.

Microsoft (at its founding): A computer on every desk and in every home.

Australia Department of Health: Better health and wellbeing for all Australians, now and for future generations.

LinkedIn: To create economic opportunity for every member of the global workforce.

The Walt Disney Company: To entertain, inform and inspire people around the globe through the power of unparalleled storytelling, reflecting the iconic brands, creative minds and innovative technologies that make ours the world's premier entertainment company.

Facebook: Connect with friends and the world around you on Facebook.

1.3 Your Mission (How)

AWARENESS

A mission statement is a powerful, customer-focused statement that clearly defines what business you are in, what makes your organization unique, and how you plan to achieve your vision.

Example:

In our restaurant example, the restaurant is good at making

tasty, healthy meals. Their mission statement is "We create and distribute great-tasting, healthy, organic meals".

ACTION

The following actions will help you define your mission statement:

- Get to know what makes you unique in the eyes of your customers. (see *WHAT ARE YOU GOOD AT?*)

- Define a mission statement that clarifies the business you are in. (See *DEFINING YOUR MISSION STATEMENT* and *EXAMPLES OF MISSION STATEMENTS*)

- Your purpose, vision, and mission are all interrelated. Revisit your definitions for each to make sure they are interrelated and work together.

- Continuously publish and communicate your mission to employees, customers, and other relevant stakeholders.

- Determine what it is that you do that is *not* aligned with your mission and realign where necessary.

- When you have a significant decision to make, go to your mission statement and ask whether the decision is in line with the organization's mission. If the decision is not aligned, you could be making a decision that will drive your business away from its core purpose. Is this what you want?

- Continuously work on upgrading your organization's core skills, ensuring that you remain best-in-class, and keeping them relevant to a changing marketplace.

- Update your one-page strategy statement.

WHAT ARE YOU GOOD AT?

To establish a mission statement, you must understand the value your organization adds to your customers. Think about what you are really good at. A word of warning, your customers might have a different opinion as to what you think you are good at.

Start by defining your core competencies. Core competencies are what give an organization one or more competitive advantages when delivering value to its customers. An organization can be considered to be a collection of core competencies.

Core competencies have the following characteristics:

- They are the source of significant competitive advantage.
- They uniquely identify the organization.
- They are widespread throughout the organization. They are not embedded in any one person who could leave.
- They are difficult to copy.
- They are difficult to identify or define since they are often a combination of technologies, processes, and culture.

Ask your customers for their view. Begin by categorizing your key customers into groups and selecting some of them to interview. Ask them what they believe your core competencies to be. What differentiates you from your competitors, from their point of view?

After you have completed your interviews, ask: What is it that you do that differentiates your organization from your competitors? How are you different? Identify where and in what functions or activities you add value to customers.

Review what you have found and define your core competencies.

DEFINING YOUR MISSION STATEMENT

Once you have defined what you are good at, brainstorm:

- Why will customers buy from you? What value do you provide? What unique benefits do you provide?

- Where has your organization been successful or made money historically? Why is this? What are your strengths?

- What passion are you trying to satisfy by building this organization?

- Describe your ideal customer.

Use your answers to define the first draft of your mission statement. Clearly state what line of business you are in and what makes you unique, from your customer's point of view. State how you intend to achieve your vision by building on what makes you unique. Avoid generalities and focus on the current organization and not what you think it *could* be. Avoid using future-driven statements like "We strive to be…". Instead, say, "We are …". A mission statement should ideally be between six and ten words. Ask yourself: Does this mission statement support your vision?

If your mission does not support your vision, then rewrite the mission statement.

Get someone to read your draft back to you. Then, write a second draft, and possibly even a third one.

When you are happy with your mission statement, discuss it with core members of your management team. Ask for their input and amend it accordingly.

When you are happy with your mission statement, go out there and share it with as many people as possible.

EXAMPLES OF MISSION STATEMENTS

Some examples of leading mission statements include:[7]

Life is Good: To spread the power of optimism.

sweetgreen: To inspire healthier communities by connecting people to real food.

Patagonia: Build the best product, cause no unnecessary harm, use business to inspire and implement solutions to the environmental crisis.

American Express: We work hard every day to make American Express the world's most respected service brand.

Warby Parker: To offer designer eyewear at a revolutionary price, while leading the way for socially conscious businesses.

InvisionApp: Question Assumptions. Think Deeply. Iterate as a Lifestyle. Details, Details. Design is Everywhere. Integrity.

Honest Tea: To create and promote great-tasting, healthy, organic beverages.

IKEA: To create a better everyday life for the many people.

---

7   Lindsay Kolowich Cox, 27 Truly Inspiring Company Vision and Mission Statement Examples, Hub-Spot, <https://blog.hubspot.com/marketing/inspiring-company-mission-statements>.

Nordstrom: To give customers the most compelling shopping experience possible.

Cradles to Crayons: Provides children from birth through age 12, living in homeless or low-income situations, with the essential items they need to thrive – at home, at school and at play.

Universal Health Services, Inc.: To provide superior quality healthcare services that: PATIENTS recommend to family and friends, PHYSICIANS prefer for their patients, PURCHASERS select for their clients, EMPLOYEES are proud of, and INVESTORS seek for long-term returns.

JetBlue: To inspire humanity – both in the air and on the ground.

Workday: To put people at the center of enterprise software.

Prezi: To reinvent how people share knowledge, tell stories, and inspire their audiences to act.

Tesla: To accelerate the world's transition to sustainable energy.

Invisible Children: To end violence and exploitation facing our world's most isolated and vulnerable communities.

TED: Spread ideas.

1.4 Your Goals

You have defined the core components of your strategy – your *vision*, *mission*, and *purpose*. To achieve your strategy, you will need *goals* and *objectives*.

AWARENESS

Goals, like a nautical compass, help set direction by defining broad primary outcomes for your organization. They are strategic, abstract, broad, intangible, and general.

To ensure the success of the organization, goals must be clearly defined and cover all core functions. (See *DEFINING GOALS*)

Typically, you will want to define between three to five characteristics, conditions, or variables that impact the effectiveness, efficiency, and viability of your organization directly and meaningfully. These could include: increase profit margin; increase efficiency; increase market share; improve customer service; improve employee skills and qualifications; or reduce carbon emissions.

Example:

The owners of the restaurant want to increase sales. To achieve this, one of their goals is to *increase market penetration*.

ACTION

The following actions will help you to define your goals:

- Define the goals necessary to achieve your vision. (See *DEFINING GOALS*)

- Publish your goals and ensure that all employees understand what they are and how they will drive future success.
- Update your one-page strategy statement.

DEFINING GOALS

Start by listing what you want to accomplish in the next year, including:

- Looking at where you have been successful in the past and capitalizing on these successes.
- Identifying lessons you have learned from past mistakes.
- Addressing your current weaknesses.
- New ideas that you want to act on.
- Where you want to add value to your customers, employees, stakeholders, or community.

Next, define what is critical to achieving your vision. These should be from across your operations and could include:

- Marketing and sales: revenue, sales performance (number of accounts, new customers, repeat business), the effectiveness of advertising, and gross profit generated per salesperson.
- Financial performance: revenue, gross profit, net profit, cash flow, and balance sheet efficiency.
- Operations: processing efficiency, service levels, shipping time, error/scrap rate, equipment efficiency, safety, unit cost, and quality.
- R&D: R&D project success rate, new product success rate, design productivity, and cost reduction.

- Human resources: staff turnover, compensation, morale, training, and overtime.

- Owner/CEO: financial reward, hours worked per week, vacation days taken, retirement planning, and personal growth.

Once you have completed the above exercises, choose three to five key goals for your organization to achieve. Summarize each goal as a statement.

Ask yourself: Will this goal help to achieve your vision? Does each goal align with your purpose statement? Are there any other potential goals that are more important than those selected?

Discuss your goals with your management team and amend them if necessary.

1.5 Your Objectives

AWARENESS

Objectives are mile markers for measuring your progress in achieving your goals. Built on top of your goals, they are tactical, specific, concrete, narrow, and measurable. You would typically have between three and six objectives.

Objectives need to be SMART (Specific, Measurable, Attainable, Realistic, and Time-based). If an objective does not meet SMART requirements, chances are you won't be successful at achieving it.

Some examples of objectives include:

- Increase gross profit margin from 27% to 30% by the end of the financial year.

- Increase efficiency by 15% by the end of the financial year (assuming you can measure your efficiency).

- Increase market share by moving from third position in the market to second by the end of the financial year.

Example:

One of the restaurant's goals is to *increase market penetration.* Their objective linked to the goal is *to increase sales by 25% by the end of the financial year.*

ACTION

The following actions will help you to define your objectives:

- Define the objectives necessary to achieve your goals. You might find that you have more objectives than goals.

- Select the top three to six objectives.

- Make sure these objectives are relevant to growing your organization and that they are SMART.

- Design a simple but effective means of tracking performance in achieving your objectives.

- Publish your objectives and ensure that monitoring their achievement is included in your performance pack.

- Regularly track performance in achieving your objectives and take corrective action where necessary.

- Update your one-page strategy statement.

1.6 Your Strategies

Without *strategies* and *tactics*, you cannot implement your strategy. Strategies are generally longer-term in nature (one year and longer), while tactics are shorter (quarterly). In this module, we will define the high-level guiding strategies essential for implementing your strategy.

AWARENESS

A strategy is about how your organization will win. It answers the question: "What will make this organization successful over time?" Ask yourself: How will the organization be built and managed? How will the organization capitalize on market opportunities? How will critical problems be solved? Your strategies will help you determine the configuration and allocation of resources to meet customer and stakeholder needs.

Strategies need to address both internal and external influences on your organization, with a key input being a SWOT (Strengths, Weaknesses, Opportunities, and Threats) analysis.

Keeping an organization on track requires following a defined set of strategies. Guidelines for a good strategy include:

- Simplicity: Aim to make a potentially complex subject simple.

- Focus: Clarify what is essential to run and grow the organization successfully.

- Readily understandable: Clearly address all major issues applicable to all stakeholders.

- Versatility: A tool that can be used for communication with multiple audiences.

- Consistency: The message is the same across the entire strategy.

- Flexibility: Easy to change, update and expand.

Example:

The restaurant wants to increase sales by 25% by the end of the financial year. One of their strategies to achieve this is to *initiate an extensive social media advertising campaign.*

ACTION

The following actions will help you to define your strategies:

- Undertake a SWOT analysis. (See *SWOT ANALYSIS*)

- Define your strategies. (See *DEFINING STRATEGIES*)

- Publish your strategies and let everyone know what it is you are trying to achieve.

- Ensure that you monitor the achievement of your strategies in your performance pack.

- Update your one-page strategy statement.

SWOT ANALYSIS

SWOT = Strengths, Weaknesses, Opportunities, and Threats. Strengths and weaknesses are *internal* to the organization, while opportunities and threats are *external.*

Strengths are what the organization is good at. They could include an experienced sales force, easy access to proprietary products, an established quality brand, or a fantastic reputation. They are not a growing market or new products.

Weaknesses are what the organization is not good at. This could include excessive reliance on one person, limited or no access to financial resources, or a lack of differentiation in the marketplace.

Look at your organization internally. Review your current operations in light of your vision and ask yourself:

- What currently works well? What has made you successful? How can you improve or capitalize on these successes?
- What critical issues are limiting your organization's growth and profitability?
  - What are the issues for each problem area?
  - What is the root cause of each problem?
  - What needs to change?
  - How will the change be measured?

Opportunities and **threats** arise from your market- and macro-environments.

The *market environment* includes your customers, competitors, suppliers, distributors, and labor force.

The *macro-environment* includes:

- Economic factors that may influence the amount of money you or your customers will have, such as interest rates, fuel prices, and inflation.
- Technology factors that impact how you produce, distribute, sell, or market your products. Disruptive technologies – such as those enabling Uber and Bolt – are a prime example of this.

- Political-legal factors, including legislation on minimum wage, employment conditions, and pollution, and the country's attractiveness to foreign investors.

- International factors that could impact how or where you do business, including global factors that could impact raw materials availability, supply chain reliability, labor markets, government regulations, and consumer dynamics.

- Demographic factors that affect the composition of the workforce or your customer base, including trends in population size or density, age structure, birth and mortality rates, and sex ratios.

- Ecological factors and how responsible your organization is to the environment.

Undertake research. What do your industry leaders do? What are their strategies? What are the key strategies for success in your industry? What trends are apparent that will impact your organization? What potential regulations or legislation changes could impact your organization?

Define your strengths, weaknesses, opportunities, and threats.

Do this exercise with your management team and other key employees. Remember that new hires and younger members often see things that management, who are often stuck in their ways, don't.

DEFINING STRATEGIES

What strategies should you define to take advantage of or to mitigate the results of your SWOT?

Make a list of your strengths, weaknesses, opportunities, and threats in a format similar to the diagram below. Choose what you feel is the most important in each area, limiting yourself to two or three options.

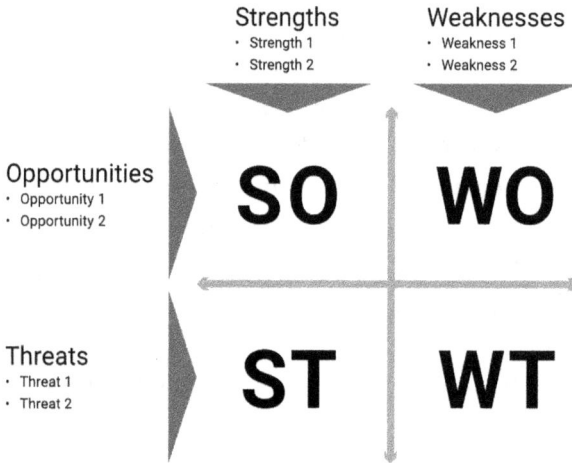

Strengths
· Strength 1
· Strength 2

Weaknesses
· Weakness 1
· Weakness 2

Opportunities
· Opportunity 1
· Opportunity 2

Threats
· Threat 1
· Threat 2

SO **WO**

ST **WT**

SWOT Analysis Template

When you are done, you will have all the information you need to start defining your strategies.

The best opportunities available to your organization are those you can exploit using your strengths, as represented in the SO quadrant above. In our example, one of our restaurant's strengths would be making food, while an opportunity exists for *Uber Eats* to deliver their meals directly to people's homes. Their strategy might be to exploit this opportunity by partnering with *Uber Eats* and launching an extensive social media marketing campaign.

Exploiting opportunities using your strengths will provide the greatest probability of success. Similarly, you would want to mitigate against the threats that match your weaknesses in the WT quadrant. Our restaurant might have a weakness in that they rely quite heavily on their chef to produce meals. A threat (in our example) could be a country-wide shortage of good chefs. Their strategy might be to ensure that the chef remains in their employ through incentives while simultaneously developing understudies.

It gets a bit more complicated when an opportunity is matched with a weakness (the WO quadrant). You may need to develop or acquire the required skills to exploit the opportunity. In our restaurant example, the opportunity could be a demand for organic food. The weakness could be a lack of secure supplies of organic produce. The strategy could be to secure the organic pipeline through partnership agreements with farmers.

In the ST quadrant, a strength and a threat are matched. Strategies often involve "buying" your way out of the threat, sometimes calling for strategies like price wars or extensive marketing campaigns. Many organizations lack the resources for such strategies.

Using the same team that defined your SWOT and your strategies, take each of the strategies you have defined and review them. Ask yourself:

- Do the strategies define how the organization will be built for you to meet your vision?

- What impact will your strategies have on your existing organization?

- Do you have the leadership, management, and other skills in your organization to deliver the strategies?

Adjust your strategies accordingly.

1.7 Your Tactics

AWARENESS

Tactics are the means of achieving a strategy. Your strategy informs and directs your tactics. Tactics are measurable micro-strategies (both in terms of results and impacts) that are actionable over a short period.

Tactics ensure that strategies are implemented. A strategy without tactics won't be executed, compromising the likelihood of achieving your vision. However, resources are finite, so you must choose the best tactics within limited resources.

Example:

One of the restaurant strategies is to initiate an extensive social media advertising campaign. A tactic related to this strategy is *to undertake a Facebook advertising campaign designed and initiated by the end of quarter 1.* This tactic would be broken down into detailed plans and actions, including available resources, the person (or people) responsible, and deadlines.

ACTION

The following actions will help you to define your tactics:

- Appoint people or teams to each strategy and work out what needs to be done to implement it through defining tactics. The people responsible for implementing the tactics should ideally be the ones leading the process.

- Define your tactics in terms of action-oriented plans, responsibilities, and timelines to implement. Capture them in a project management app or tool.

- Design a simple but effective means of tracking performance in achieving your tactics.

- Regularly track performance and take corrective action where necessary.

- Review your tactics regularly – at least quarterly.

2

Culture and Values

It's people who make a great organization, and they are an integral part of your strategy. Your culture is the core component driving people dynamics, of which values are a subset. This module discusses ways to influence your culture and values.

2.1 Your Culture

AWARENESS

The culture of an organization is its *personality*. It originates internally and impacts how things are done. It is made up of shared beliefs, behaviors, and values. It is based on a strongly held and widely shared set of beliefs across the organization. It defines behavior, allowing employees to respond appropriately in any given situation.

Culture is expressed through:

- The organization's values.

- The degree of urgency to respond to any situation.

- How the individual is valued. For example, a task-driven organization places emphasis on the task and often has set methods to complete that task. People-oriented organizations focus on the individual and value individual input into how things should be done.

- The level of hierarchy. Often, the higher the level of hierarchy, the slower the organization is to respond.

- Its structure. Certain functions within a structure might have higher status – and therefore greater priority – over other functions.

Organizations that manage their culture positively significantly outperform those organizations that don't. Managing your culture can result in successful differentiation from your competitors, resulting in greater revenue growth and profits (*See GREAT ORGANIZATIONAL CULTURE*). Disengaged employees, poor customer relations, and high staff turnover are all symptomatic of an organization that does not manage its culture, or manages it poorly. Such behaviors generally have a negative impact on profitability.

It is the leader's role to recognize, understand, and manage the organization's culture to ensure optimal organizational performance. You (and your leadership team) directly impact your organization's culture through your beliefs and actions.

What people do matters more than what they say or believe. The leadership team must, therefore, be aligned in your beliefs and demonstrate the desired culture daily.

Culture is difficult to measure and is consistently evolving. While culture is difficult to change – and should never be changed too rapidly – you can, and should, manage your culture. Changing an organization's culture is done through changing behaviors. These changed behaviors will influence and change the organization's culture over time.

GREAT ORGANIZATIONAL CULTURE

Every organization has a different culture that helps it to retain its uniqueness. High-performing organizations have the following distinct cultural qualities that set them apart from other organizations: [8]

- *Alignment:* The organization's vision, purpose, goals, and objectives – and its employees – are all pulling in the same direction.

- *Appreciation:* All team members frequently provide recognition and thank others for their contribution.

- *Trust:* Team members feel safe to express themselves and are supported by other team members, especially when trying something new.

- *Performance:* Individuals are motivated to excel, thus contributing to profitability and results.

- *Resilience:* Being able to watch for and respond to change with ease.

8   Kellie Wong, Organizational Culture: Definition, Importance, and Development, 2020, Achievers, <https://www.achievers.com/blog/organizational-culture-definition/>.

- *Teamwork:* There is collaboration, communication, and respect between team members.

- *Integrity:* Rely on fellow employees to make decisions, interpret results, and form partnerships – with honesty and transparency.

- *Innovation:* The organization capitalizes fully on available technologies, resources, and markets while applying creative thinking to use these to impact performance positively across all aspects of the organization.

- *Psychological Safety:* Employees are encouraged to take risks and provide honest feedback. This starts at the team level rather than at the individual level.

ACTION

Changing an organization's culture is a slow process. It can take several years. You will have to work within your current culture because it is how your employees currently behave.

There are three key steps to follow in changing culture: *communicate, take action,* and *recognize.*

The following actions will help in changing your culture.

- Start by identifying your ideal culture and how it differs from your current culture. (See *CREATING AN EN-TREPRENEURIAL CULTURE* and *DESIGN THINK-ING CULTURE*)

- Identify elements of your current culture that you can use to get to your desired culture. For example, you might have a culture of working hard, but you also want to become more customer-centric. How can you use this hard work ethic to promote your customer-centric requirement?

- It is easier to change behaviors than mindsets. Identify where current behaviors drive the culture you *do not* want. Look for behaviors that are tangible, actionable, repeatable, observable, and measurable. Small behaviors have a large knock-on effect. For example, insisting on a clean workplace can have a knock-on effect of improving quality assurance.

- You might have a long list of behaviors that require improvement, but focusing on too many will dilute your efforts and, in all likelihood, result in failure. Narrow your focus and choose two or three behaviors that you can focus on rigorously. Aim at initiatives that can demonstrate impact quickly and implement them. Once you have implemented these changes, you can move on to other behaviors.

- Ask your employees to provide input. When they feel part of the process, they are more likely to accept the changes. Find ways to involve them in identifying problem areas and defining solutions. When asking for input, make sure you are listening and that you plan to act on their suggestions. Don't sabotage your efforts through a lack of attention.

- Aim at codifying the new behavior into simple, practical steps that can be practiced daily.

- Review your operational procedures to ensure they are aligned with the changes you are making. Include your culture in your onboarding process. Ensure that external communications are aligned with your desired culture. Make sure your performance management process is aligned to your desired culture.

- Make sure the behavior you want is linked to achieving your business objectives.

- When introducing the concept, focus on emotions. You want to personalize your employees' experience so that they will feel good about the new way of doing things, making success more likely.

- You might want to start with a pilot study. Carefully select a small group of employees to test the new approach on. If it is successful, it will be easier to spread the concept throughout the organization. You can use the members of your pilot study as team leaders when rolling the changes out to the rest of the organization.

- Use training and development to make sure your employees know what is expected of them.

- Recognize – and excel in recognizing – improvements. Recognition is extremely powerful and should be used frequently. Recognition can also be financial in the form of bonuses or increases. Make sure that all methods of recognition are aligned with your organization's values.

- Publish your results. Use appropriate methods to get the word out there that the behavior change is producing results.

- Ensure that your culture is reinforced in all areas of your organization. Ask yourself: Are your organizational processes aligned to your culture? Do you include culture as an element of your reward and recognition systems?

- Leadership by example is critical in changing culture. Ensure that your behavior – and that of your leadership team – is aligned to your desired culture and values.

- Use your informal leaders – those who are not in leadership positions but have influence in your organization – to help define and embed new practices. Be mindful of not making them feel manipulated into doing so – you don't want them to be against the change you require. Ask your employees who the informal leaders are if you are not sure.

- Keep your culture in mind when interviewing new employees. Ask questions designed around cultural fit. Reinforce your culture during the onboarding process.

- Culture changes continuously. Actively monitor and manage it on an ongoing basis. Business circumstances also change continuously, and your culture might need to change to meet these new challenges.

CREATING AN ENTREPRENEURIAL CULTURE

When creating and building your organization, you needed to be entrepreneurial. Over time, and as your organization has grown, it might have lost its entrepreneurial flair. The following key steps will help you to find, support, and nurture entrepreneurship.[9]

1. **Break the Silos**

   As organizations grow, they tend to develop silos often around their various structures. This goes against entrepreneurship. Many companies are not short of ideas – they simply lack the entrepreneurial risk-taking spirit and passion they once had for bringing their ideas to market.

   Ask yourself:

   a. Has your organization developed silos that stand in the way of developing an entrepreneurial spirit?

---

9   Sangeeta Bharadwaj Badal, 2012, Building Corporate Entrepreneurship Is Hard Work, Gallup, <https://news.gallup.com/businessjournal/157604/building-corporate-entrepreneurship-hard-work.aspx>.

b. Does your organization develop great new ideas? Do they get to market? Why not?

c. Do you encourage the risk-taking necessary to get new ideas to market?

d. Do you have people with the passion to drive new ideas to market? What is stopping them?

e. Can you develop cross-functional teams to generate brilliant ideas and get them to market quickly?

2. Identify and Foster Talent

Not everyone has the natural talent to be a successful entrepreneur or innovator.

a. Do you have employees who are natural entrepreneurs?

b. Are you developing them as entrepreneurs, or are you discouraging them?

c. What can you do to encourage their entrepreneurial abilities for the betterment of your organization?

d. How can you continue to attract employees with entrepreneurial abilities?

3. Create the Right Environment

Create the right environment to foster your entrepreneurs. This includes:

a. An environment that is open to risk-taking. You need to tolerate failure and accept change.

b. Encouraging trusting relationships. Trust encourages employees to take risks without the fear of losing their jobs if something goes wrong.

c. Building skills and knowledge. Offer opportunities

to learn and grow. Support new ideas and initiatives driven by your employees.

d. Offering support. Be committed to innovation, open to change, and prepared to delegate authority appropriately. Send a clear message that the organization is serious about creating an entrepreneurial environment.

e. Providing resources. Provide entrepreneurial projects with sufficient resources, time, and material to be successful.

f. Maintaining a supportive organizational structure. This starts with the strategy and includes the management hierarchy. While systems, policies, and procedures are established to bring about order and control, they may constrain entrepreneurial activity. Identify practices that discourage entrepreneurship and look at ways of changing them. Simplify approvals, cut red tape, and keep things flexible.

g. Set performance goals with realistic timelines and performance measures. Design reward systems that accommodate failure, with a focus on long-term outcomes.

4. Continually Assess the Environment

Take the time to continuously review your organization's progress toward having an entrepreneurial culture. Ask your employees about their views on the organization's culture. Does their day-to-day environment encourage entrepreneurial thinking and action? Does management foster an entrepreneurial environment?

Here are some quick steps to take to help you on your way:

- Allow employees to experiment with low-risk opportunities.
- Listen to new and younger employees. New employees often see things from a fresh perspective. Younger employees often find quick and easy ways to get around frustrating problems and come up with novel ideas.
- Recognize and reward employees for innovations.
- Provide the resources and budget to implement ideas.
- Every now and then, force your staff to think creatively by setting unreasonable goals. Remember, there is no such thing as a mature organization, only mature managers who lack creativity and do things the way they have always been done.

DESIGN THINKING CULTURE

Traditionally, there are two prevailing (but opposing) business philosophies. There is **analytical thinking,** which involves rigorous quantitative analysis. According to this philosophy, activities need to be continuously repeated according to a set method to ensure standardization and profits. Then, there is **Intuitive thinking**, which allows for creativity and innovation. Both approaches have their strengths and failings. *Analytical organizations* tend *not* to see the next trend and only adapt when it is too late. *Intuitive organizations* often don't get their act together to fully capitalize on their opportunities.

Design thinking[10] is a third approach that allows analytical thinking and critical thinking to co-exist within an organization. Organizations that encourage, explore and exploit both approaches increase their chances of success.

The knowledge funnel below outlines the core concepts behind design thinking.

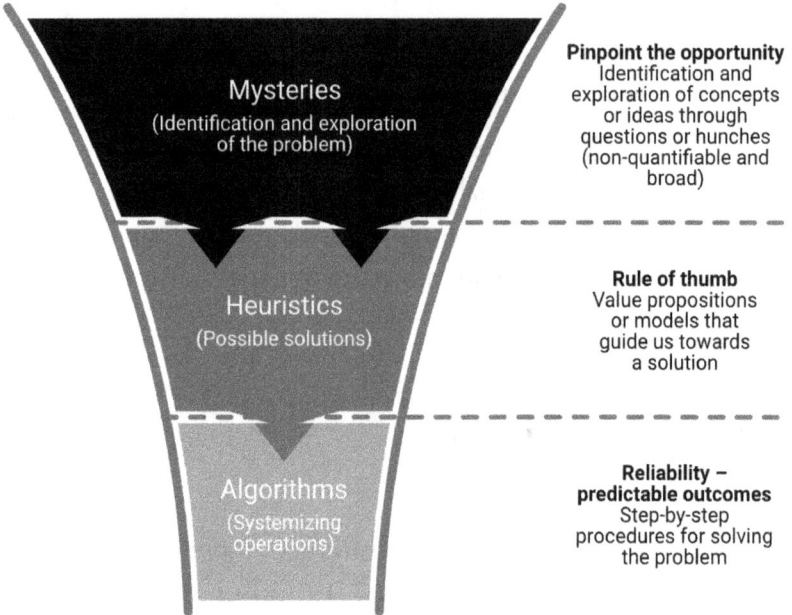

The Design Thinking Knowledge Funnel

The first stage of design thinking is the **Mysteries** stage. A mystery is a new idea, opportunity, or concept. At this stage, the mystery enters the funnel and is open to exploration. For example, a doctor might want to explore how to lessen the negative impacts of chemotherapy on a patient; an entrepreneur might explore providing quick, convenient, tasty meals; an

---

10   Roger L. Martin, The Design of Business. Harvard Business School Press, 2009.

agricultural researcher might look at determining ideal planting times and methods, or a scientist might wonder why objects fall to the earth at different rates.

The second stage is the **Heuristic** stage. It is where the problem is defined, and a solution designed, developed, and demonstrated. You might apply a rule of thumb to narrow the mystery into manageable-sized issues that need resolving. In the Heuristic stage, an organization looks at how it can use its intellectual capital and competitive advantage to capitalize on possible solutions. For example, the doctor might look for a more people-centered approach to treating chemotherapy patients; the entrepreneur might develop a quick service, drive-through restaurant; the agriculture researcher might develop an improved method for planting that caters for different environmental circumstances, and the scientist might determine that it is a force called gravity that causes an object to fall.

The final stage is the **Algorithms** stage. It is where systems and procedures optimize the execution of solutions defined in the Heuristic stage. The solution is perfected and geared up for repetitive and cost-effective use. For example, the doctor could introduce a new protocol for treating chemotherapy patients that can be applied in oncology units across multiple hospitals; the entrepreneur could open a chain of fast-food restaurants eventually across the world; the agriculturist could develop an app that helps farmers determine what crops to plant depending on their location and climate conditions, and the scientist could define a number of rules that explain the force of gravity.

Using the funnel requires two key activities: **exploration** and **exploitation**. *Exploration* (seeking new knowledge) is the key activity required to transition successfully between the different stages of the funnel. *Exploitation* (maximizing the payoff) is the key activity within each stage of the funnel. Typically, organizations will master either exploration or exploitation and then only focus on that. To get the most out of the knowledge funnel, organizations need to focus on exploration *and* exploitation.

The knowledge funnel balances the exploration of new knowledge (innovation) with the exploitation of current knowledge (efficiency). It helps explain how organizations identify opportunities, develop solutions to these opportunities, and then determine a means of fully exploiting these solutions to add value to the organization.

A successful organization must continually look at moving through the different stages of the funnel. Even when an organization has successfully exploited a successful algorithm, they must push themselves back into the Mysteries stage to ensure that they stay ahead of the game anticipating changes to user needs and the competitor landscape.

McDonald's is a prime example of an organization that went through each of the three stages and perfected the algorithm: They identified the need for fast foods (Mysteries); they developed a business aimed at meeting this need (Heuristic); and they perfected the delivery of fast and cheap food through standardization (Algorithm). However, in the 1990s, they became so focused on implementing their algorithm that they missed the consumer swing to healthier food, losing market share in the process.

Every organization has constraints – be that a lack of capital, impossible customer demands, or suppliers trying to squeezing too much out of a deal – which can be seen as limiting factors. Design thinking practitioners see constraints as opportunities. For design thinkers, constraints make solving the problem challenging and exciting. Constraints make finding different – and often better – solutions possible. Seeing constraints as opportunities rather than as the enemy is a simple change in mindset that can result in great opportunities for your organization.

When introducing a design thinking culture within your organization, you may encounter resistance.

The three main obstacles to overcome when introducing a design thinking culture are:

- A historic reliance on analytical thinking and reliability. Most business training is based on inductive and deductive logic, and your employees will, in all likelihood, have been extensively trained to be analytical thinkers. Logic has been reinforced throughout people's working lives, with intuitive, creative thinking squashed at every opportunity.

- Key stakeholders want reliable results, which are often focused on the short-term. Reliability and short-term focus are enemies of intuitive thinking.

- It is easier to defend analytical thinking and reliability than design thinking and validity. Analytical thinking is based on what was, and people generally find it easier to support results based on the past rather than on new possibilities. Design thinking is based on what could be, which is a difficult concept for analytical thinkers.

Review how your organization operates:

- Is your organization typically analytical, intuitive, or design oriented?

- What are the long-term sustainability impacts of this focus on your organization?

- Is this the best approach to achieve your vision?

- What do you need to do to change your organization's focus and approach?

2.2 Your Values

AWARENESS

Values are the fundamental beliefs that guide your organization and its behavior. They are the guiding principles that your organization uses to manage itself, both internally and externally. They define the organization's identity or fundamental character. Values can set an organization apart from its competitors.

Values have become a "tick box" requirement for strategy definition, a dream that, once defined, is ignored until the next strategic planning session. Most value statements are generic "motherhood-and-apple-pie" statements that add no value to the organization. For example, I know of an organization whose values are truth, accountability, respect, growth, excellence, and trust. These values are displayed on walls through the organization but not one person (when asked) was able to tell me what the organization's values were. They are all good statements but they are meaningless. No one lives by them and they do nothing to provide a competitive edge. Such ineffective statements often serve to demotivate employees, alienate customers, and undermine management credibility.

Values can have the advantage of:

- Helping with the decision-making process where an activity or product does not live up to a value.

- Providing a competitive edge.

- Educating customers about the purpose of the organization.

- Attracting and retaining key employees.

Defining and sticking to meaningful values is hard work and takes commitment. They require constant work to ensure that they are successfully applied in an organization. Values can create tensions in an organization – for instance, an employee might feel left out; potential strategic decisions might conflict with the values; operational freedom might be constricted; and management might be open for criticism in areas where their actions contradict their values.

Patrick M. Lencioni, in his Harvard Business Review article, *Make Your Values Mean Something*,[11] identifies four types of values – core values, aspirational values, permission-to play values, and accidental values:

- *Core values* guide all actions. They should never be compromised. They are sustainable, timeless and do not change.

- *Aspirational values* are those needed in the future but that are currently lacking. They should not dilute the current core values.

- *Permission-to-play values* reflect the minimum behavioral and social standards required of an employee. They are generally the same for companies across a region or industry. They do not help distinguish an organization from its competitors.

- *Accidental values* arise unconsciously without being specially cultivated and come about as a result of common interests

---

11   Patrick M. Lencioni, Make Your Values Mean Something, Harvard Business Review, 2002, <https://hbr.org/2002/07/make-your-values-mean-something>.

and personalities. While they might create an atmosphere of inclusivity, they may, in contrast to core values, have a negative impact on the organization.

Values are a set of fundamental, strategically sound beliefs that are *imposed*. Value setting is not a consensus activity. Management must continuously live by and reinforce the organization's core values – it is a powerful tool for driving culture. If you are unwilling to commit to doing this, it would be advisable *not* to have a values statement.

ACTION

Define your organization's values using the following actions:

- Select a small team of employees or members of management, including the owner or CEO, who have a comprehensive understanding of the organization, are high performers, and are well respected within the organization.

- Ask everyone to read up about values. Lencioni's article is a good starting point.

- Ask the group to list what they believe to be the core values of the organization. Document these as verbs and not nouns – nouns are not actionable. (See *EXAMPLES OF VALUES*)

- Ask the group to review the values against Lencioni's four categories of values. Keep only the *core values* and make sure there are no generic motherhood-and-apple-pie statements.

- Ask:

  • Will these values provide a competitive edge?

- Would you want the organization to hold these values if, in the future, they become a competitive disadvantage?

- Are the values timeless?

- Communicate your chosen values to your employees. Print a copy for each employee.

- Build your values into all core processes, including customer communications, recruitment, performance assessment, reward and promotion, and decision-making.

- Again – continuously communicate the values and make sure everyone lives by them. Employees should be continually reminded of the core values.

- Are your core suppliers / service providers aligned with your values? If not, should you consider finding alternate suppliers?

EXAMPLES OF VALUES

Some values often found in organizations include:

- People-oriented with a focus on fairness, respect, and tolerance of the individual.

- Outcome-oriented with an emphasis on achievements and results.

- Team-oriented with a focus on collaboration.

- Innovation-oriented with a focus on creativity and experimentation.

- Task-oriented with an emphasis on analytical thinking and precision.

- Design thinking-oriented with an emphasis on creating a balance between innovation and analytics.

- Entrepreneurially oriented with an emphasis on change and risk-taking.

- Stability-oriented with an emphasis on security and following a predictable course.

- Aggressively oriented with an emphasis on competition.

2.3 Renewing Your Organization

AWARENESS

In the business world, change is ubiquitous, but most organizations have a deeply embedded resistance to change. Change can be extremely disruptive. It is often easier to be mediocre than to change to best practice.

Change in organizations is usually driven either by a crisis or by a change in leadership. Having the energy to change is difficult, especially when not driven by either of these two. The dilemma for leadership is, do we continue serving our customers in the way we always have, or do we instigate change to keep ahead of the pack? It is not an easy dilemma to resolve.

The downside of not managing change can result in lower productivity, passive or active resistance, higher employee turnover (and the loss of key people), increased absenteeism, increased conflict, reverting to old practices, project failure, and ultimately, performance decline.

While change is usually defined at the organizational level, *actual* change occurs at the individual level. For change to filter throughout the organization, each employee needs to go through their own journey to the end picture.

Leading by example is the most effective method of helping employees understand what is important. Employees take their example from the leadership team. Top management's role is about doing and not just saying. If management has a zero-tolerance policy for poor quality, this will reflect in employee performance. Allowing poor quality to sneak through the process will send a message that it is okay to be sloppy.

When initiating change, start in an area where you would most like to see a change in performance. What feeling do you get in the work environment? Does it drive the performance you want? For example, the work area might be stuffy or dark, or you might notice that the layout of the cubicles is impeding workflow. What is the managerial style like? For example, the managerial focus might be compliance-driven, while customers might require flexibility. What kind of overall impression does the work environment create? Is it energizing, or is it dead? Don't be limited to these questions – review all aspects of the work environment. You can only start addressing change once you know what and where the problems are.

Leadership's challenge is to create a culture of change while not dropping the ball. Change needs to take place while maintaining the integrity of core products and services. This is not an easy balance to achieve.

John Kotter[12] defined eight phases of succeeding with change in an organization. The eight phases are:

---

12   Kotter, John P. Leading Change. Boston, Mass: Harvard Business School Press, 1996.

Creating a climate for change	1. Create urgency for change
	2. Form a powerful coalition to drive change
	3. Develop a vision for change
Engaging & enabling	4. Communicate the change vision
	5. Empower your people to change
	6. Create quick wins
Implementing & sustaining	7. Build on the change
	8. Make it stick

Kotter's Eight Phases of Change Management

The approach laid out in Kotter's eight-step change model is particularly important when implementing projects that fundamentally change the way work is done, such as introducing a new business system.

ACTION

The following actions will help you renew your organization:

- Identify the areas you want to change. Describe the current situation, the desired situation, and where you are likely to be if change is not effected.

- Determine how easily change can be implemented. Some changes require a change in leadership. Other areas need a comprehensive change process – for example, the introduction of new technologies. List the forces that will assist change and those that will resist change. Score each of the forces to determine which will be the most useful in implementing change and those that need to be addressed to ensure that change happens. Use this understanding in your change process.

- Define a change process. A comprehensive change process could look something like this:

  - **Create a Climate for Change**
    - o Determine the urgency with which you need to change (changing market, competition).
    - o Understand the nature and extent of the change and who is impacted.
    - o Determine who is going to drive the change and then empower these individuals to do so.
    - o Identifying any risks that the change might bring to the organization.
    - o Develop tactics to facilitate change.
    - o Define your vision for change and develop strategies to achieve the vision.

  - **Manage Change (Engaging and Enabling)** (See *RESISTANCE TO CHANGE*)
    - o Develop communications strategies and share the vision.
    - o Ensure that the leadership is behind the change, that they share a common purpose, and that they are role models for change.
    - o Develop training that enforces change.
    - o Use coaches to drive individual change.
    - o Determine how resistance is going to be managed. Empower people to clear any obstacles that might be blocking change.
    - o Identify, celebrate and reward quick wins.

- **Reinforce Change (Implementing and Sustaining)**
  - Encourage, celebrate and reward change.
  - Build on growing credibility while gradually changing all systems, structures, and policies that don't fit in with the vision.
  - Hire, promote and develop individuals who embrace change.
  - Reinvigorate the change process with new projects, themes, and change agents.
  - Continuously improve performance across all areas of operations and management.
  - Use audits and employee engagement to ascertain whether the change has been effective.
  - Develop plans to correct issues.
  - Lead from the front. Make sure you change your behavior to enforce the change you require. Your employees will look to you to see how seriously *you* practice the change.

RESISTANCE TO CHANGE

When meeting any form of resistance, relying on logic will most likely get you nowhere. You need to appeal to people's emotions if you want them to change.

There are several ways to deal with resistance to change:

- *Education and communication:* Prepare people for change in advance through communication and education. Be open and honest in your approach to pre-empt rumors based on inaccurate information.

- *Participation and involvement:* Involve employees in the change design process, particularly where they have the required detailed knowledge or where they could become centers for resistance.

- *Facilitation and support:* Support your employees during the difficult times of change through training, coaching, and counseling.

- *Negotiation and agreement:* If an individual or a group of people believe the change is going to find them at the short end of the stick, you will need to enter into negotiations with them. You could give resisters specific roles (for example, in the decision-making process) or incentives (for example, severance packages) during the change process.

- *Manipulation and co-operation:* This should only be used when other tactics are not working or are too expensive. You could co-opt the resisters onto the change team, not for their contribution but for the sake of appearance. Be mindful that this can backfire and lead to greater resistance if those co-opted feel that they are being used.

- *Explicit and implicit coercion:* This should only be used as a last resort and might include making it clear that resistance to change could lead to job losses, transfers, holds on salary increases, or promotions.

3

Leading the Team

To start an organization, you need to be entrepreneurial. To grow your organization, you need to be a leader. Not all entrepreneurs are natural leaders. *Leadership* is about inspiring your people to achieve the organization's vision, and encouraging and supporting them to achieve beyond their expectations. *Management* is about allocating responsibilities, monitoring performance, and taking remedial action. It is often extremely difficult for one person to play the role of leader and manager, both from a personality perspective and because of conflicting roles. It isn't easy to inspire people to greater heights when you are planning to give them a below-average salary review six months down the line.

There are some basic skills that you can apply that will go a long way in developing your leadership skills. Before you begin, and if at all possible, you might want to consider splitting the management role from the leadership role and appointing someone to take responsibility for the daily management of the organization.

What are the fundamentals of leadership?

1. Setting the future *vision* and *strategy* for the ongoing success of the organization.

2. Ensuring *execution* by building the systems to deliver the results.

3. *Managing* employees through engaging, motivating, and communicating.

4. *Developing* employees through formal and informal processes.

5. Ensuring *proficiency* by creating trust, acting with integrity, being attuned to people and their needs (social and emotional intelligence), and by making decisions.

In this module, we will consider how effective you are as a leader, and provide skills for effective leadership.

No one person can do everything necessary to grow an organization. At some stage, the entrepreneur will employ people to help them deliver their vision for the organization. As the organization grows, the entrepreneur relies more and more on employees to develop the organization. Teamwork is an excellent method to achieve results through your employees.

No intervention or renewal is possible without using a change management process to align your employees with the required changes. We will look at assisting your interventions through change management.

Finally, we look at you, the owner or CEO, and the influence you have on the organization and your support networks.

Adapted from Jason Barron's *The Visual MBA: A Quick Guide to Everything You'll Learn in Two Years of Business School.*[13]

3.1 Leadership and Delegation

AWARENESS

As an organization evolves from being an owner-operated organization to one needing managers, the owner's role also evolves. Owners need to transition to a leadership role while letting go of day-to-day operations to enable continued growth. Organizations often encounter problems when distributing effective power and decision-making to managers because managers don't always share the same perspective as the business owner about the organization.

The challenge for the business owner is to have a clear vision for the entire organization while ensuring that the operational managers align people and resources with the organization's strategy. To do this, the owner needs to delegate. Effective delegation is not just about allocating a set of tasks to someone but rather about delegating responsibility for the delivery of a particular function or outcome. This can involve:

- Redefining the roles of the owner and delegating some of these roles to managers.

---

13   Jason Barrow, The Visual MBA: A Quick Guide to Everything You'll Learn in Two Years of Business School, Penguin Business, 2019

- Clearly defining and communicating performance expectations, goals, standards, and priorities.

- Reviewing processes such as planning, budgeting, and decision-making, while setting clear limits on authority and the ability to commit resources.

- Finding the right people to fulfill the managerial roles, either from within the organization or externally.

Author Paul Hersey, and leadership expert Ken Blanchard, who developed the Hersey-Blanchard Model[14], suggested that what is most important is for a leader to adapt their leadership style to the situation at hand. Their situational leadership model envisages four primary leadership styles catering to the different levels of experience and ability of employees:

1. **Instructing:** A new employee will typically have high levels of commitment but low levels of expertise. They need strong leadership. The leadership style to adopt is one of instructing.

2. **Coaching:** The employee's level of expertise has increased, but motivation and commitment might have fallen owing to stress or familiarity with their job. The employee begins questioning while looking for answers themselves. The leadership style to adopt is primarily that of a coach.

3. **Supporting:** The employee's skill level has risen sharply, but motivation can vary from one employee to another. Employees with declining motivation might have resigned, or their motivation might have increased as they take on a greater role and become more independent. The relevant leadership style to adopt here is one of support.

---

14   Hersey, Paul and Kenneth H. Blanchard, Management of Organizational Behavior: Utilizing Human Resources. Englewood Cliffs, NJ: Prentice Hall, 1993.

4. **Delegating:** The employee is in full control of their work and is highly motivated. They might be given projects to run with and teams to lead. The leadership style to adopt with this type of employee is one of delegation.

The COVID-19 pandemic enabled the growth of virtual offices, but remote working brought with it new challenges for leaders. The demand to work remotely is likely to remain after the pandemic is over. Refer to *THE VIRTUAL OFFICE* box below for tips on leading and managing your employees remotely.

ACTION

The following activities will help to improve your leadership and delegation:

Know your strengths

Do you know your greatest strength? Most people think they know their strengths, but they are usually wrong. Knowing your strengths is perhaps one of the most important things you can do for yourself.

Management guru and author Peter Drucker used a simple technique to help him better understand his strengths. Whenever he had to make an important decision, he wrote down what he expected to happen. A year later, he compared what he expected to happen with what *actually* happened and reflected on the results. In this way, he got to know himself better and found ways to improve. He got to know his strengths and how to manage his weaknesses.

The type of information you might want to capture when keeping track of your decisions includes the choices you make, the results you expect, why you expect things to pan out a particular way, and how you feel about your decision.

Inspiring vision

Leadership is defined by having a clear understanding of why you are in business, clear values, and a core philosophy. Inspiring leaders:

- Develop and live an enabling vision.
- Work with internal and external stakeholders to make the vision a reality.
- Support and encourage the attainment of the vision and what needs to happen to get there daily.
- Live the organization's vision. They share it with everyone daily. They discuss with employees how their work is contributing toward helping the organization to reach its vision.
- Find ways to improve their trust in their people. Leaders expect their people to trust them, but they must trust their employees before this can happen.

Lead by example

Employees are boss-watchers. How you spend your time (and who with) will become the organization's preoccupation. Your actions send powerful messages to your staff, including the stories you tell or the people you invite to meetings.

Here are some ways to lead by example:

- Lead by personal example. Focus your time on the organization's top strategic priorities.

- Your day-to-day decisions reflect your commitment to the vision, and your behavior shows your commitment. Review your vision and determine how you can reinforce it daily through your routine activities.

- Understand the symbolic significance of each of your acts. Understand the power of small actions.

- Make sure all your decisions reflect the organization's vision and strategic priorities.

- Always behave ethically, especially when emotions are running high. Emotions often lead to short-term thinking. Remember who it is that you want to be, and when in doubt, ask yourself: "Would I be happy if the decision I am about to make ends up on the evening news?" If not, then don't do it. For any decision, especially one that is emotionally charged:

  - Instead of reacting immediately, stop and think.

  - Gather facts and information. Is it critical to make a decision now? Who is (or should be) involved? What is at stake?

  - Brainstorm solutions to come up with the best alternative.

  - Make a decision while asking yourself whether or not the decision is ethical.

Manage your time

To be a truly effective leader, determine what is important and what is not. Using *The Eisenhower Method*[15], effective time management looks at two dimensions in determining priorities: relative importance and urgency. To determine your priorities:

---

15   Mikael Krogerus and Roman Tschäppeler, The Decision Book: Fifty Models for Strategic Thinking, Profile Books, 2017.

- List all your issues and tasks.

- Rank these tasks according to their importance. Importance can be High or Low.

- Rank these tasks based on their urgency. Again, use High or Low.

- Determine your priorities. The figure below summarizes your options.

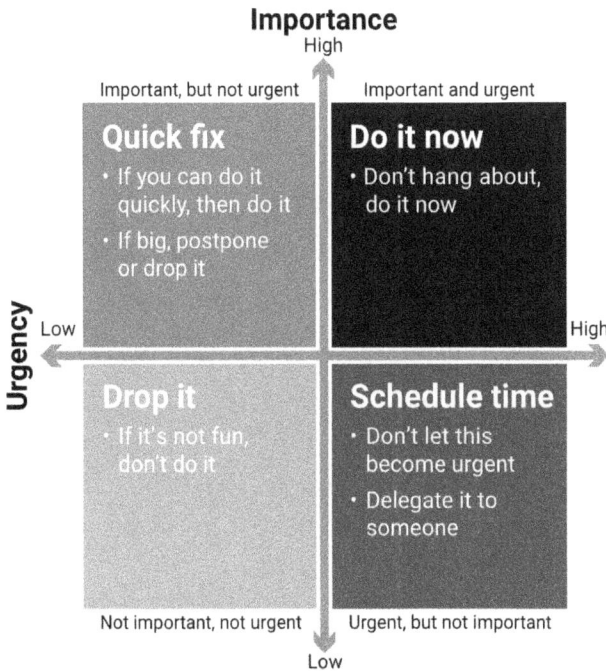

Importance
High

| Important, but not urgent | Important and urgent |

Quick fix
- If you can do it quickly, then do it
- If big, postpone or drop it

Do it now
- Don't hang about, do it now

Urgency Low   High

Drop it
- If it's not fun, don't do it

Schedule time
- Don't let this become urgent
- Delegate it to someone

Not important, not urgent   Urgent, but not important
Low

The Eisenhower Matrix

- Having only two dimensions (High and Low) can be considered naïve. Once you are using the model effectively, you can design a more comprehensive rating method that suits you.

- Managing your time might only be part of the problem. Are you managing your energy? In many instances, managing your energy is more important than time management. Make sure you take breaks, exercise, and relax to maintain your performance levels.

Visible management

- Practice visible management. Lead where the action is, where the customer is, where the new competitor is, and where the disgruntled dealer is.

- Reduce information distortions.

- Consider getting rid of your office.

- Be ever-present. Develop your employees through training, coaching, cajoling, caring, and comforting.

- Visit your staff in their offices instead of expecting them to come to you.

Pay attention

- Become a compulsive listener. The best way to engage people is to listen to them. Listen to their frustrations and then act to change the situation.

- Listen constantly, consolidate ideas, share ideas and information, and recognize achievement. Develop formal and informal methods to enable you to listen (for example, surveys, chats, regular get-togethers, newsletters, celebratory events, and personal thank-you's). Ask yourself: Are you listening or telling? How open are you to new ideas?

- Visit all areas of your organization regularly. While there, interact with your employees.

- When engaging with employees, think of yourself as a consultant wanting to know how things work or don't work.

- Build trust by keeping your promises and demonstrating that you genuinely trust and care about your people.

Defer to the front line

- Ensure that the front-line people – the implementers, the executors – know they are the heroes. Spend time with them.

- Honor the support functions to the extent that they support the front-line people.

- Only promote people who create excitement among their people and colleagues, as well as those who reward subordinates' accomplishments.

Delegate

You cannot do everything yourself. Delegate by:

- Identifying the correct person to delegate to. Meet with that person to explain the purpose of the meeting and why you have chosen to delegate to them.

- Describing the new task and responsibility. Explain how the new task and responsibility will affect them and their overall job.

- Asking the employee for their response to the new task and responsibility. Discuss any points they might raise.

- Agreeing on responsibilities and performance expectations and empowering them to be self-managed.

- Asking the person to document what they think you have asked them to do, how they intend to handle it, and how they plan to do it.

- Reviewing the plan and offering your support. Provide coaching and mentoring where necessary.

- Leaving them to get on with the job in a controlled manner. Start the concept small and test what is needed to make it successful. This is how you prove that you trust them.

- Celebrating their successes. Take corrective actions where necessary.

Bashing bureaucracy

- Take the lead in destroying all forms of bureaucracy in your organization.

- Manage across functions. Don't allow functional structure get in the way of delivering effective customer solutions.

- Encourage working together to solve customer problems. Banish internal competition and encourage collaboration.

Love for change

- Regularly ask yourself what you and your subordinates have recently changed.

- Each meeting should start with what has been changed since the last meeting.

- Communicate successful changes regularly.

- Develop a love for change, and focus on improving your performance.

- Take the lead in destroying all forms of bureaucracy.

Sense of urgency

- You want the organization to be energetic. Encourage speed and change.

- Instill a sense of urgency throughout the organization.

- For each action, ask yourself how it will be perceived across the organization. Will it create urgency, will it be neutral, or will it be "business as usual"? You want to encourage urgency.

Some of the above pointers have been adapted in part from Tom Peters' *Thriving on Chaos*[16] as well as Peter Wilson and Sue Bates' *The Essential Guide to Managing Small Business Growth*[17].

Leadership and design thinking

It is easy for an organization to focus on its short-term goals. In doing so, there is a natural tendency to focus more on analytical thinking results, such as compliance with systems and procedures. Typical management and measurement systems enforce the analytical thinking focus.

It is the responsibility of the CEO to continuously promote both the exploitation (or reliable administration) and the exploration (or invention) of the organization, providing a balance between the two. Highly successful CEOs may specifically take it upon themselves to drive innovation within their organizations.

How do you become a design thinking leader?

Start by looking at yourself. Where do you stand concerning analytical thinking versus intuitive thinking? Depending on the

---

16   Tom Peters, Thriving on Chaos. Alfred A. Knopf, 1987.

17   Peter Wilson and Sue Bates, The Essential Guide to Managing Small Business Growth, Wiley, 2003.

results, determine what you can do to strengthen your skills in areas of weakness. If you are predominantly analytical, what can you do to downplay your need for reliability and to enhance your intuition? What can you do to increase your knowledge?

To be design thinking-oriented, you need to develop three specific skills:

1. Become good at observing. Look around you. What do you see? Is an employee struggling to comply with an outdated process? Is a customer frustrated with a product? Ask yourself questions like: is there something fundamentally wrong with the way our organization sees the market? What practices do you encourage through the questions you ask or the reports you require? Could you ask things differently and get different results?

2. Develop your imaginative skills. Read, daydream, talk to people, and play more. Develop your imagination.

3. Develop solutions to the issues you have noticed during your observation and imagination. Free up time and capital to examine and resolve your organization's challenges.

You can develop your expertise in design thinking by reflecting on what you have experienced. Consider whether you have adequately integrated analytical and intuitive thinking, reliability and validity, and exploitation and exploration.

Learn to say no

It is necessary at times to say no, even though it can be difficult to do. If you struggle to say no, these pointers might help:

- Review the request and avoid responding impulsively. Understand where the request is coming from. Does it align with where you want to be? What time and effort is involved? Is it your job? Who should be doing it?

- When saying no, be firm in your reply. Be courteous and give a brief explanation of why you are saying no. Don't offer weak excuses, and don't beat about the bush.

- Offer advice or guidance on how to go about resolving the request. For example, you could offer to help coach the person so that they can do the work themselves.

Making decisions

- How do you make decisions? There are various approaches to decision-making. Some are covered below in the *DECISION-MAKING* box.

DECISION-MAKING

When making decisions, it is important to remove emotion from your decision-making. Quantitative and qualitative screening can be useful since it provides data to help you make a decision. Here are some approaches to help you:

METHOD 1: GO OR NO-GO DECISION

Let's say you want to launch a new product. You have done your initial research and business case, and everything seems to be pointing in its favor. You are at the point where you need to decide whether you are going to take it forward or not. What follows is a stepped approach to help you make your decision.

Step 1: Define about five quantitative and qualitative criteria against which you are going to measure the product. These could be strategic requirements (must-haves), operational objectives (wants), restraints or limits. Before you go any further, review your criteria by asking why you chose them.

In our example, the criteria could be the need, whether the product can be sold to existing customers, profitability, speed to profit, and team capability.

Step 2: Estimate the potential of the new product against the criteria by using a simple scoring method:

- If the answer is *high*, score the criterion with a 3.
- If the answer is *medium*, score it with a 2.
- If the answer is *low*, score it with a 1.

Be careful with your scoring. If, for instance, you set *getting to profit quickly* as a criterion, and you envisage a quick turnaround for the project, then your score for *getting to profit quickly* would be *high*, thus scoring a 3. The quick turnaround could lead you to believe that the time period is low (and that the score should thus be a low). This would be wrong and would distort the result.

In our example, the scores could be as follows:

The need	High	3
Will it sell to existing customers?	Medium	2
Profitability	High	3
Speed to making a profit	Medium	2
Team capability	Medium	2

Step 3: After scoring the criteria, add up the scores and average them. In our example, our total is 12. Since we have five criteria, divide the total by 5. Our average score is 2.4.

Step 4: Analyze your results. Since 3 was the top possible score, you would want your average to be as close to 3 as possible. Look at the average you have calculated. Look at the criteria and their scores. Is the product launch such a good idea? You might decide that a score of anything less than 2.5 is just not viable.

Since our score falls short at 2.4, suddenly the new product does not look quite as attractive. We might need to look at what has made it fail the test and determine whether the situation can be rectified before completely abandoning it. For example, employing a skilled operator might push the team capability factor to 3 and the average to 2.6.

METHOD 2: CHOOSING BETWEEN ALTERNATIVES

In this method, you have a problem that needs solving, and there are several ways to solve it. How do you decide which is the best alternative to solving the problem? You might want to increase your fitness levels, but you're not sure where to begin because of the many alternatives available.

Step 1: Define the problem. Spend some time correctly defining the problem. Don't rush this step – you don't want to be solving the wrong problem inadvertently. For example, is the problem "the best method to get fit" or "the best gym to join"? If we choose the problem as "getting fit", there are more potential solutions.

Step 2: Define the criteria against which you are going to score the project. Define about five quantitative and qualitative criteria against which you plan to measure your alternatives.

Before reviewing your criteria further, ask why you have chosen them.

For "getting fit", your criteria might be ease of facilitating exercise, variety, cost, being outside, and having fun.

Step 3: Brainstorm alternatives. Come up with as many viable options for solving the problem as possible. This is an important step, so spend time on the alternatives.

In our example, we might have brainstormed: joining a gym, running in a forest, swimming in the sea, and employing a personal trainer.

Step 4: Estimate the potential of each alternative against the criteria. Use a simple scoring method:

- If the answer is *high*, score the criterion with a 3.
- If the answer is *medium*, score it with a 2.
- If the answer is *low*, score it with a 1.

	Criteria and Score										Total
	Ease		Variety		Cost		Outside		Fun		
Gym	Medium	2	Medium	2	Medium	2	Low	1	Low	1	8
Running	High	3	Medium	2	High	3	High	3	High	3	14
Swimming	Low	1	Low	1	High	3	High	3	High	3	11
Trainer	High	3	High	3	Low	1	Medium	2	High	3	12

Be careful with your scoring to ensure that it reflects what you are trying to achieve. In our example, a high cost would receive a low score because you might have a limited budget.

Step 5: Now that you have scored each alternative against the criteria, add up your totals for each alternative.

Step 6: Analyze your results. The alternative with the highest score is the alternative that could offer the best results in solving the problem. In our example, *running in the forest* is the best solution.

Step 7: Up until now, the approach assumes that all criteria are equally ranked. You might feel that this is naive and that the some criteria should carry more weight than others. To do this you could add complexity using a 1-2-3 scale again, where 3 is the highest ranking criteria and 1 the lowest. You would then multiply your criteria scoring against the criteria weighting. A high criterion score of 3 and a high ranking of 3 would give a total score of 9.

A word of warning: complexity does not always provide a better answer. This model is simple in design, and the scoring is subjective. You might be surprised when the simple scoring method provides the same answer as a more complex approach.

Now it's time to add some complexity by weighting the criteria. *Ease* and *Cost* are the most important criteria and weigh in at 3. *Variety* is not important and has a weighting of 1. The remaining criteria all have a weighting of 2. The scores from the table above are multiplied by the weighting factor to provide the following results:

		Criteria and Score					Total
	Ease	Variety	Cost	Outside	Fun		
Weighting	3	1	3	2	2		
				Results			
Gym	6	2	6	2	2		18
Running	9	2	9	6	6		32
Swimming in the Sea	3	1	9	6	6		25
Having a Personal Trainer	9	3	3	4	6		25

The results stay the same after weighting, with *running in the forest* as the preferred option, and *swimming in the sea* and *having a personal trainer* coming in at a joint second.

METHOD 3: INTUITIVE DECISION-MAKING

You are down to a choice of two, but you cannot make up your mind. Rationally, you have added up all the advantages and disadvantages but are confused because of all the data and cannot make a call. Your quantitative and qualitative analysis has resulted in a tie. You now need to rely on your intuition.

How do you tap into your intuition? A simple method is to flip a coin. Decide on what face of the coin (heads or tails) represents which decision. Then flip the coin.

While the coin is still spinning in the air, you will, in all likelihood, want it to land a certain way. Your intuition is telling you the decision you would like. You don't even have to look at the coin as you have your intuitive answer.

These decision-making models have been adapted from Mikael Krogerus and Roman Tschäppelar's *The Decision Book – Fifty Models for Strategic Thinking*, and Jason Barron's *The Visual MBA: A Quick Guide to Everything You'll Learn in Two Years of Business School*.

THE VIRTUAL OFFICE

The COVID-19 pandemic opened up opportunities for working remotely. Working remotely is not strictly working from home but rather away from the office. The extent of working remotely depends on the type of work you do but applies to nearly all organizations. Here are some pointers to ensure that remote working is successful, both for you and for your employees.

LEADERSHIP

There are two critical points to get right when leading remote-working employees:

1. Focus on outcomes rather than on the amount of time spent doing the job.

2. Trust and empower your employees.

With your focus on outcomes, your emphasis is on results and not on time spent doing the work. What is important here is the *quality* of work done. If an employee can do their job to the required standard in half a day, so be it.

If you cannot trust your people, there is probably something wrong with your recruitment process. Trust your people to do their job but also empower them to do it by:

- Getting to know your people and their individual circumstances. Show that you care.

- Communicating outcome expectations and timelines.

- Making sure your employees know what they are doing each day.

- Setting clear guidelines about what is expected of your employees regarding response times to communications and queries, and attendance at meetings and webinars.

- Spending time coaching people to be more productive.

- Trusting your employees by allowing them to set their work place and times. This may, however, be dictated by customer expectations.

- Enabling your employees to explore new ideas, take educated risks, and make mistakes.

- Praising people when they get things right and recognizing a job well done. This is something that is easily forgotten when you are not in regular physical contact with your employees. Make extra effort to show your people that you appreciate their work.

- Be constructive in your comments, even when people get things wrong.

- Don't micromanage, and don't bring in draconian rules when the majority are doing a good job and you are only let down by a few.

By focusing on outcomes and trusting and empowering your employees, your expectations might very well be exceeded. You could be surprised at how well your organization thrives under this type of leadership approach.

TEAMS

Teamwork under remote work conditions is essential for your organization. To get this right:

- Structure your organization into teams to do the required work. These should be small and cross-functional, depending on the work they will be doing. Such teams need to be designed to enable quick decision-making and to be able to operate independently.

- Make sure each team has the necessary technology and skills to do their work.

- Make sure that the teams have clear reporting lines and decision-making authority. They also need to know who to include in intra-team discussions, when necessary.

- Set each team's weekly outputs and goals. Teams might require daily tasks and goals with daily meetings. These daily activities should be managed internally by the team.

- Team leaders need to manage communication actively and to provide feedback to team members.

- Team leaders must prioritize and promote a healthy team culture. Much of the organization's culture will develop through teams. Culture is a feeling of connection between co-workers created by similar priorities, interests, and attitudes. Each team will need to work out how to work best.

YOUR PEOPLE

Introduce new ways of ensuring that your employees can work remotely effectively, such as:

- Making sure they have the right set of skills to work remotely.

- Helping them to manage the stresses associated with working remotely.

- Relooking at your codes of practice. For example, do you need to remind your staff about the confidentiality of information when working in a public space or when disposing of reports?

- Determining whether your staff has a dedicated and ergonomically sound workspace. You don't want to see an increase in time off to treat injuries from, for example, incorrect posture.

- Hosting regular events to bring people together so that they can connect and develop relationships. Set these up well in advance.

- Developing a mentoring or support program to help employees overcome the sense of loneliness that may arise from working remotely. Mentoring is going to be particularly important as you bring on new employees.

- Review your recruitment and onboarding process to determine how to adapt it to cater for remote hiring, onboarding, and training of employees.

TECHNOLOGY

By the time you read this book, you probably would have resolved many of the technological problems associated with working remotely. Since the initial disruptions of the global shutdown, there have been many enhancements and improvements to what was available at the outset. There have also been new challenges:

- Your employees will require sufficient bandwidth and hardware (for example, a laptop) to enable their working remotely.

- Not all the software your employees are used to accessing at the office will be available to them remotely. You might need to find alternative ways of providing your employees with access to the software they need.

- While your existing means of communication and project management might have worked when everyone was in one location and they could easily get up and talk to each other, you may want to consider investing in additional software to help manage teams working remotely. There are new software solutions that help to cater for some of that missing ongoing human interaction as well as helping in the development of a remote work culture.

- Remote working has brought with it an increase in cybercrime. Your remotely working employees may have compromised your cybersecurity inadvertently. Make sure you have the best security you can afford, supported by backup plans.

- Your information technology (IT) advisors might push certain software solutions for technology-driven reasons. Before deciding on any solutions, explore newer technologies – like video conferencing solutions – that provide an improved user experience compared to what traditional service providers are offering.

DIGITAL SKILLS FOR YOUR EMPLOYEES

There are a number of key skills that you and your employees must perfect to ensure success in the digital world.

1. **Collaboration and Communication Skills**

   While, in the past, you may have walked over to a colleague to discuss a point with them in a face-to-face environment, digital literacy has placed new demands on the way we communicate. It is important that you are able to express yourself (and your intentions) fully in writing or while engaging in webinars without the back and forth of direct contact. Writing skills training (for example, writing effective emails) and training in digital communications platforms (for example, webinar conduct and etiquette) are essential in the digital era.

2. **Online Etiquette**

   Do your employees know how to behave during, for example, a webinar? We might have witnessed incidents like an attendee visiting the bathroom during a webinar (and forgetting to turn their video off), but there are many other nuances, such as being on mute, talking over people, and camera positioning to look professional.

3. Managing Online Identities

Your employee's profile on, for example, social media reflects their personal brand. In an increasingly digital world, the boundaries become blurred between the employee's personal brand and that of the organization for which they work. Customers are not always able to distinguish between the two. Your employees will need coaching and direction in terms of managing their digital profiles. The more professional their brand, the better the impact on the organization's brand.

4. Continued Learning

The digital revolution is accelerating. Things that were not even considered possible a number of years ago are now everyday practices. Organizations that don't manage the impacts of the digital revolution on their operations, will probably not survive. Similarly, as individuals, we must ensure that our own and our employee's digital skills remain relevant through continual upskilling.

5. Digital Literacy

You and your employees need to become literate in many areas to remain relevant in the digital world. These include:

- ICT (information and communications technology) literacy: We should be open to adopting new technologies as they develop.

- Information literacy: We should be able to source, collate, store, evaluate and share data and information in digital format.

- Media literacy: We should be able to produce professional-looking content for distribution to a wider audience, both within and external to the organization.

HELPING REDUCE EMPLOYEE BURNOUT

Working remotely can cause employees stress, burnout, and even pessimism. You can help to reduce these stresses by holding an end-of-week meeting where you ask each person to answer four questions. You can even add these questions to an existing meeting. Ask everyone to answer each question before moving on to the next question:

- Share an example of at least one success from this week.

- What was your biggest frustration from this week?

- What accomplishment are you most proud of from this week?

- What is one lesson from your successes this week that you're going to bring into next week?

Asking about successes contributes toward increasing optimism and its associated health benefits. Optimistic people are more likely to give their best effort at work. When people are burned out, they are more inclined to be negative and to focus more on their failures than on their successes.

Work frustrations can cause employees to be demotivated and to underperform. Listen carefully to how your employees respond to this question. You need to get to the bottom of frustrations as quickly as possible and to rectify the situation. Other attendees may be able to help by suggesting solutions.

The next question deals with personal accomplishments and what the employee did personally. Accomplishments come about when the individual feels they are in control of their own success or failure. People are happier when they feel in control of their personal situations.

The final question is about building on successes. It is about building the employee's ability to meet the challenges ahead. When an employee believes that they are empowered to tackle challenges head-on, it will make a significant dent in potential burnout.

By spending a little time at the end of each week asking these important questions, you will find that your employees are less frustrated, burned out, and pessimistic, with a corresponding improvement in engagement and performance.

Adopted from *Forbes Magazine* July 12, 2020

3.2 Teamwork

AWARENESS

Teamwork is a highly effective means of improving performance. Teamwork is all about co-operation between those who are working on a task for the betterment of the task as a whole.

"Team" is an overused term. It is often used to name a group of people doing similar work or having the same boss. Effective teamwork occurs when a group of people cooperate and support each other in pursuit of a common purpose. The objective of a team is to achieve more together than the same number of people working would achieve working separately.

Delegating work to teams is often a challenge for a business owner. It means letting go of the reigns and trusting the team to do their job. While doing so would have been counterintuitive when establishing the organization, learning to delegate is essential when growing the organization.

Teamwork is fundamental for teams to work effectively. Only when the skills and strengths of individual team members are combined to achieve a shared vision will the benefits of a team be apparent. The attitudes and behavior of the each team member is essential to the success of the team.

Effective teamwork attributes include:

- Trust in team members to deliver what they promise.
- Willingness to help when needed.
- Sharing of a common vision for the project or work undertaken.
- Co-operation and using each other's strengths.
- Positive attitudes and providing support and encouragement.
- Active listening.
- All team members pulling their weight – and in the same direction.
- Giving others the benefit of the doubt.
- Consensus building.
- Effective conflict resolution.
- Open communication.

Adapted from David Hall and Dinah Bennett's *The Hallmarks for Successful Business.*[18]

---

18   David Hall and Dinah Bennett, The Hallmarks for Successful Business, Management Books, 2002.

ACTION

The following actions will help to improve your teamwork.

- Organize as much as possible around your teams. Look at what work you do or at work that can be completed with projects. Ask yourself: What can be better delivered using a team?

- Start the concept small and test what is needed to make the team successful. Take one of the identified areas that could be managed by a team; then define the problem and the outcome you would like to see.

- Identify the team. Discuss with the team what you want from them and the boundaries within which they need to work. Such boundaries include decision-making responsibilities and authorizations, progress reporting, timelines, and quality management.

- Empower the teams to be self-managed. Allow the teams to flourish without you. Your interference with their work will destroy the concept of delivering through teams. Your teams have to feel truly empowered to do what is right to grow the organization.

- Problems may arise when a supervisor previously managed the work you have now delegated to a team. You might need to manage the changing role of the supervisor. Such a person can sabotage the team concept if they feel undermined and excluded from the process.

- Ask your teams how team working could be improved. Identify problems, determine solutions, and agree on actions. Review your team's performance (See *TEAM PERFORMANCE*). Take action and follow up.

- If you feel the output is not what you expected, arrange for an expert external to the organization to review your teamwork to ascertain what is working and what needs improvement.

TEAM PERFORMANCE

Is your team capable of delivering to the level necessary to meet your strategy?

The model below will help you to assess your team's performance as individuals and to identify where you are missing team skills to deliver your strategy.

Start by defining the skills and expertise that are necessary for the team to deliver. These could be hard skills (for example, technical, business, or sales knowledge) or soft skills (for example, people skills, going the extra mile, and motivation). Go through the list of skills you have identified and reduce them to those skills that are necessary to get the job done. Ideally, identify between five and eight skills. Ask yourself why you have chosen those skills.

Take the skills and define what an acceptable level of performance is. For example, social media knowledge might be a core skill. An acceptable level of performance around this skill might be a good working knowledge of Facebook, LinkedIn, and Twitter. Link the acceptable level of performance to a 10-point scale, with 10 being fantastic, 5 being acceptable, and 1 being very poor). Score each team member against these skills.

The graph below provides an example where there are five skills identified for team success: sales, technology, teamwork, creativity and interpersonal. The team consists of four members each of which have been scored against the required skills.

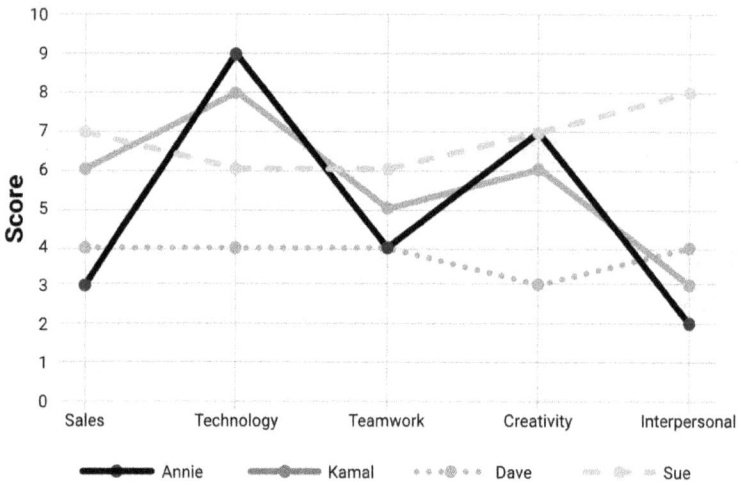

Team Performance

From a team perspective, it is now easy to identify where the team lacks core skills. In the example above, the team is short in interpersonal skills and teamwork. Sue is good at interpersonal skills and could balance out the others. She should be tasked with leading sales initiatives. The weakness in teamwork is concerning since this is a project that requires teamwork. Intervention is most certainly needed here.

One of the assumptions behind forming teams is that no one person can be an expert in all the areas required for optimal delivery. You need to bear this in mind when you look at individual performance.

In our example, Dave is below performance in all areas. You have to ask why he is part of the team. Annie's performance is all over the place and she could be considered a poor performer.

However, her technical performance is off the charts. Despite her poor showing in the majority of areas, her technical abilities are key to the project's success. Annie needs to be encouraged and developed in her role despite her other scores.

Adapted from Mikael Krogerus and Roman Tschäppelar's *The Decision Book – Fifty Models for Strategic Thinking.*

3.3 Owner Influence

AWARENESS

The owner's personality has a direct impact on the organization. Their strengths and weaknesses are often reflected in the organization. As a business owner, understanding yourself is critical in terms of your impact on the organization and in finding ways to maximize your strengths and mitigate your weaknesses.

Once you understand yourself, you can bring other people on board to complement your skills. For example, if you are great at developing clients but poor at administrating and managing, it might pay off to employ someone to run all aspects other than sales. This could even include employing a CEO to run the organization while you concentrate on sales.

Adapted from David Hall and Dinah Bennett's *The Hallmarks for Successful Business.*

ACTION

The following actions will help you to manage your impact on the organization:

- Ask yourself: Am I doing what I love? What can you do to do more of what you love?

- Undertake strengths- or psychometric tests. Adjust the way you interact accordingly.

- Ask key employees to appraise how well you manage. What do they perceive your strengths and weaknesses to be?

- Maximize the use of your strengths and consider ways to minimize your weaknesses. Look at delegating your areas of weakness – that are essential to the operations of the organization – to others.

- Keep a time log, recording where and how you spend your time. Capture each activity into broad categories such as strategy implementation, marketing, client liaison, people management, leading the organization, operational optimization, and administration. Review where you have spent your time, convert it into percentages, and ask whether your time is aligned with business priorities. Focus your time on where you can add the most value.

3.4 Owner Support Network

AWARENESS

Being a business owner can be lonely. A support network can be vital in supporting you and your organization. Do you use your support partners to your full benefit?

Support networks consist of individuals and entities that provide you with a necessary service but are not core to your organization. These typically include:

- Shareholders or board members.

- Employees.

- Other entrepreneurs.

- Suppliers.

- Customers.

- Professionals, including accountants, tax advisors, bankers, legal advisors, and advisors or agents (for example, insurance advisors, estate agents, and sales advisors).

- Associations, government entities, or other institutions.

One of the core but hidden support members are your immediate family and friends.

Adapted from David Hall and Dinah Bennett's *The Hallmarks for Successful Business.*

ACTION

The following actions will help you to improve your support network:

- Make a list of all people or organizations that are a key part of your support network. Don't forget family and friends. What is their primary role in being a support partner to you?

- Review your relationship with each and ask yourself if they add value, if the relationship is neutral, or whether they detract value from you and your organization.

- Identify where there are gaps in your support network. Which relationships should you terminate?

- Determine actions to make each of your networks a preferred supporter. Decide how frequently you need to be in contact with them, and then put a reminder in your diary.

- Visit each member of your support network, or show them your organization. Discuss your vision for the organization and ask how they can help you to achieve it. Decide who you can partner with and who should be replaced.

- Put essential family and friend dates and events in your diary. Make sure these events are sacrosanct and fit your work priorities around them.

4

Review Your Strategy, Culture and Leadership

Congratulations on defining your strategy and culture, and on reviewing your leadership capabilities. This is not an academic exercise – your strategy needs to be a living, breathing document that sets the foundation for your organization.

To ensure that this happens, here is a review and recap of this section:

- Review your strategy, culture and leadership. (See *REVIEW YOUR STRATEGY, CULTURE AND LEADERSHIP*)

- Publish your one-page strategy and values and distribute them widely within your organization and among your stakeholders.

- Make sure you refer to your strategy and values daily and encourage your management team to do the same.

- Make sure that everyone in your organization, and how you do business is aligned with your strategy and values.

- When you have to make a major decision, make sure your decision is aligned with your organization's strategy and values.

- Visit your tactics often (at least quarterly) and make sure that they are helping you to attain your vision.

- Capture your actions in a project management tool and monitor their implementation.

- Review your strategy annually. You will probably only make minor tweaks to it but make sure it stays relevant through regular reviews. As you get closer to achieving your vision, you will be less likely to have the continued energy to go beyond the vision. You may decide to reinvent your vision at this stage.

Now that you have defined your strategy, culture, and leadership requirements, where to next? While your strategy paints a picture of your organization's future, it is not complete and needs to be interpreted at different levels throughout the organization. The next section allows you to review your operating model in light of your strategy.

REVIEW YOUR STRATEGY, CULTURE AND LEADERSHIP

STRATEGY

You have defined your strategy. So, how good is it?

Enlist the help of someone who is independent of the strategy definition process to go through the points below to review the effectiveness of your strategy:

- The most important guidelines for a strategy are sanity, reason, and common sense. If you cannot explain your strategy in a few sentences, it might not be a good strategy. Is your strategy convoluted? Does it get lost in detail?

- Remove all buzz words (like "strategic") from your strategy. These words can disguise the substance of the strategy. Does the strategy still make sense without them?

- Don't spend too much time on the vision in your review. Getting there is far more important.

- Is your mission or purpose statement customer-focused? Your customers pay the bills, so ensure that they play a prominent part in your strategy.

- How seriously do you address your customers in the strategy? Did you talk to your customers? Who are your customers, and what are their needs? Are they addressed in the strategy? Is the strategy the best way to meet the customers' needs?

- What value do you add to your customers? Does this value-add meet their needs? Will your strategy help to deliver the value-add to the customer?

- Go through the rest of your strategy (goals, objectives, strategies, and tactics). Ask yourself what the end result of the organization will be. Can you still envisage the bright future you want for the organization? Why?

- Does the strategy clearly define your differentiators? How do you intend to exploit and enhance these differentiators?

- Is your strategy aligned with expected market developments? Avoid having a strategy that will become obsolete after six months because of changes in the market.

- Is your strategy aligned with your operating model? Can you deliver your strategy?

- Is the strategy aligned with your organization's culture? Strategy means change, and if your culture resists change, you might have challenges in implementing the strategy. *(See CULTURE below)*

- Do you have the necessary leadership team to deliver your strategy? *(See LEADERSHIP below)*

- Are the challenges clearly defined? You cannot implement a strategy without knowing the challenges you face and how you intend to overcome them.

- Does your strategy tell a new story, or is it just a repeat of what you have always done? If it is just a repeat, then you have to question its validity seriously. The market is changing continually with increasing momentum. Just because it worked in the past is no guarantee that it will work in the future.

- Are there any conflicts or trade-offs in the goals? What impact will these trade-offs have on delivering the strategy?

- When allocating limited resources, what choices have been made in terms of delivering the strategy? Ask yourself: Are these the best choices to deliver the strategy?

- Check for consistency. Contradictions and inconsistencies will not go away and will more than likely contribute to the failure of the strategy.

CULTURE

Review your culture:

- Do you understand your organization's current culture? Do you understand the shortcomings of the current culture?

- Have you identified the fundamental beliefs and behaviors necessary in your organization to achieve your organization's vision? Do you believe this revised culture will achieve the difference you require?

- What three or four initiatives are you going to introduce to change behavior?

- How are you going to implement the changes you want?

LEADERSHIP

Review the leadership within your organization:

- What style of leadership is necessary to achieve your organization's vision? Is your current leadership style appropriate? Is it better that you lead your organization, or should you rather focus on what you do best?

- Do you have the correct management team to achieve your organization's vision? What needs to change?

- How do you plan to get the most out of your team to achieve your organization's vision?

SECTION 2

WHAT YOU WANT THE ORGANIZATION TO DO

This is the second section outlined in the approach and covers **what you want the organization to do**. It is highlighted in the diagram below:

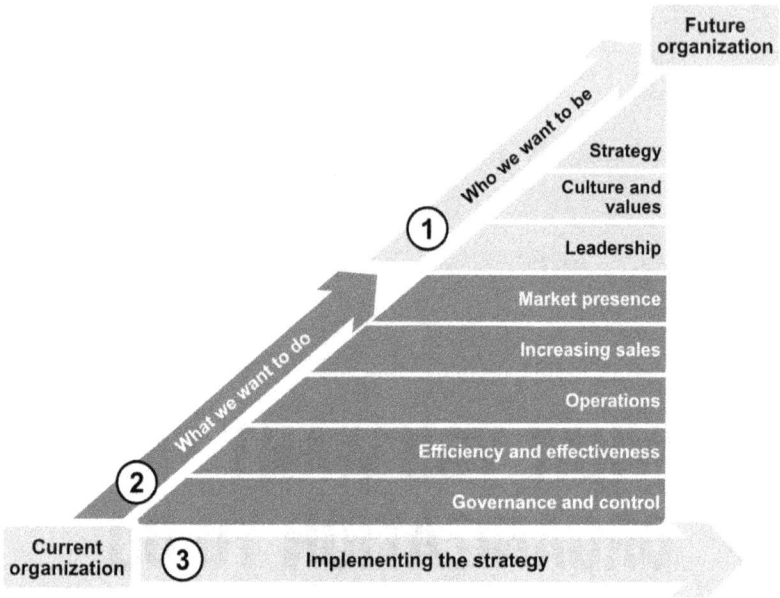

Section 2 of the Tool

An organization is organic and fluid, changing all the time to meet different internal and external circumstances.

Your strategy has defined how you intend to drive change in your organization – now, you need to change how you do business. The details of delivery are considered in this section through the following modules:

- Market Presence
- Increasing Sales
- Operations
- Efficiencies and Effectiveness
- Governance and Control

5

Market Presence

It costs more to find new customers than it does to maintain relationships with existing customers. Good customer relationships reduce your transaction costs, making your organization more profitable over time.

Marketing starts with the customer and how you intend to ensure their satisfaction with your service offering. It covers how you find, win and retain customers. Good customer marketing and relationship management are also dependent on delivery. Your operations, systems, procedures, values, and culture all need to support your customer-focused strategies. The objective is for the entire organization to be aligned when it comes to servicing the customer.

How you intend finding and servicing your customers is defined through a marketing strategy. This module examines the elements of a marketing strategy and covers target markets, brand positioning, competitive advantage, and the marketing mix. It also reviews optimizing your range of products and services through innovation.

A marketing strategy is influenced by several forces, including new technologies, economics, competitors, regulations, and societal and political forces. These forces (which are beyond the scope of this book) need to be continuously monitored to be aware of market dynamics that could impact your organization in the future.

5.1 Segmentation by Knowing Your Customer

AWARENESS

Marketing starts with a clear understanding of your customer. Group your customers into market segments as defined by their buying behavior. Researching the needs of your current and potential customers will become a key activity in your marketing efforts.

Ask yourself:

- Who is the customer?
- What do they buy?
- Why do they buy?
- Where do they buy?
- How do they buy?

Once you know your customers and have segmented them, you can define their segment profile.

ACTION

The following actions will help you to improve your understanding of your customer.

- Understand who your customer is and what their needs are. Understand their buying behavior. (See *UNDERSTANDING YOUR CUSTOMER*)

- Segment your customers according to their buying characteristics.

- Profile your customers by defining:

  - Their demographics. This includes activity, size, location, financial standing, market share, the person making the buying decision, and influencers.

  - Their psychographics or why they buy. This includes personality traits, lifecycle stage, interests, attitudes or beliefs, and activities.

  - Their buying behavior. This includes preferred products or services, reasons to buy or not to buy, factors influencing the buying decision (price, delivery, quality, service), price sensitivity, volumes purchased, purchase frequency, where the customer hears about your product or service.

  - Give the segment a name that describes it. For example, you might have a group consisting of pensioners. You could call this group "The Seniors", or something similar that is instantly recognizable.

UNDERSTANDING YOUR CUSTOMER

Answer the following questions for each of your customer segments. If necessary, undertake a customer survey to answer some of these questions. (See *CONDUCTING A CUSTOMER PERCEPTION SURVEY*)

1. Who are your customers? Who makes the buying decision? Who recommends? Who influences? Who else benefits from the purchase?

2. What do they buy? What preferences do they have?

3. Why do they buy? What benefit do they want? What does the product or service mean to them?

4. Why do they choose one product or supplier over another? Is it because of quality? Price? Service? Reliability? Convenience? Habit? Less rational reasons?

5. Where do they buy? Is it because of the place? Channels? Competition?

6. What volumes do they buy? When (and how frequently) are purchases made?

7. What prices do they pay? How sensitive are they to price changes?

8. Where does information about the product or supplier come from? What media do they read, view, or listen to, and what kind of information influences their buying decision?

CONDUCTING A CUSTOMER PERCEPTION SURVEY

1. Identify your key customers. Focus on your key 20% of customers that make up 80% of your revenue. You could also include lost customers and those you would like to do business with in the future. Aim to contact between thirty and fifty customers.

2. Contact each of your customers using the most appropriate medium (for example, by email or telephonically), explaining that you are undertaking a survey to evaluate and improve your performance. Explain that you have identified them as being key to providing you with input and that you would like to set up a telephonic interview.

3. Determine what it is that you would like to find out from them and design a questionnaire accordingly. Aim for the telephone call to be no longer than twenty minutes. Make sure that your questions are open-ended. Questions could include:

   - What do you look for in a supplier?
   - What needs are you looking to address?
   - What is the most important of these needs?
   - What disappoints you in a supplier?
   - On a scale of 1 to 10, how do you rate us as a supplier? Why?
   - What improvements could we institute to improve our service to you?
   - How frequently would you like to receive communications from your supplier?

- How can we do more business with you in the future?

4. Make sure the survey adds to your credibility with your customers. Undertake a practice survey and fine-tune your questions. How do you plan to capture and collate the results? This is a vital step. You need to have a pretty good idea of how you intend to use the results. There is nothing worse than having a large set of survey responses without knowing how to collate the information to provide meaningful conclusions. The way the answers are captured will depend on how you intend to analyze them and how many responses you expect to receive.

5. Decide if you will do the interviews in-house or find a service provider to do the survey. Consider using a web-based survey tool.

6. Prepare your interviewers. Make sure they understand what you are trying to achieve. Give them some pointers to probe answers, such as asking for examples, asking what is meant by their response, asking what other things are important. Make sure they understand how you want the results captured. You want customer responses and not the interviewer's interpretation of the interview.

7. Undertake the survey.

8. Collate the information. What are the most frequently mentioned issues? What are the customers' needs in order of priority? How is your organization perceived?

9. Based on the results, what are the priority actions you need to take to improve your position as a preferred supplier?

Adapted from David Hall and Dinah Bennett's *The Hallmarks for Successful Business*.

5.2 Differentiate Yourself

AWARENESS

Once you have segmented your customers, determine what differentiates you in each of your market segments.

To be competitive, you must differentiate yourself from your competitors in the eyes of your customer, be it through your product, the service you offer, your method of distribution, your customer relationships, your reputation, or the price of your goods and services.

To improve your service offering continually, you must be a specialist in your chosen area. You need to create new market niches continually through new products and services. Impress your customers by transforming your products or services continuously by adding more and more value (features, quality, and service). The more a product is perceived to be mature, the more opportunities there are to differentiate it through the accumulation of small advantages.

You need to be able to compete with the best. You need to understand your competitor's differentiators so that you can have strategies in place to mitigate their advantages.

Many of the available differentiators are not suitable for small- to medium-sized organizations, mainly because of the costs of fully servicing the differentiator. The two most affordable and effective differentiators available to small- to medium organizations are *customer service* and *relationships*. Look at ways of servicing your key customers better. Deliver a service that exceeds their expectations. Customers will keep coming back to you and will be advocates for your products and services.

ACTION

The following actions will help to improve your differentiation:

- For each market segment, determine what sets you apart from your competitors. Often, what you think are your differentiators are not what your customers see as setting you apart. Ask customers in each segment what they believe to be your differentiators. (See *POSSIBLE DIFFERENTIATORS*)

- What are your competitors' differentiators? (See *KNOW YOUR COMPETITORS*)

- Define a positioning statement for each of your market segments. This would include defining the target market (customer profile), distinctive competence (why customers buy from you), benefits customers are looking for, positioning statement (what sets you apart from your competitors), your positioning message (your single most important message in terms of your offer), and what you need to do to improve your differentiation within this market segment.

- In light of your positioning statement, review your branding proposition. (See *BRANDING*)

POSSIBLE DIFFERENTIATORS

The following are possible differentiators:

PRODUCT DIFFERENTIATION: ACTUAL AND PERCEIVED DIFFERENCES

- Product features meet client needs.
- Top quality performance and reliability of product.
- The product does what it says it does.
- Good durability and lifespan of product.
- Comprehensive warranty.

SERVICE DIFFERENTIATION

- Ease of placing orders.
- Quality of service staff going beyond what is required of them.
- On-time and correct delivery of order.
- Post-sales service, including installation, training, and resolving issues.

DISTRIBUTION CHANNEL DIFFERENTIATION

- Coverage appropriate to customer needs/availability.
- Expertise availability through distribution channels.
- Performance in meeting orders.
- Levels of customer or technical service.

RELATIONSHIP DIFFERENTIATION

- Trusted member of the customer team.
- Competence and approachability of customer contact team.
- Credibility of solutions proposed.
- Reliability and speed in meeting promises or fixing problems.
- Keeping the customer informed.

REPUTATION DIFFERENTIATION

- Perception – high levels of service, superior product quality, or performance.
- Ongoing brand communication – unique and different.
- Image consistency.

PRICE DIFFERENTIATION

- Lowest cost provider.

KNOW YOUR COMPETITORS

Answer the following questions about each of your competitors:

- What drives your competitor? (Their goals, beliefs about the industry, and their values and aspirations)
- What is the competitor doing? What can they do? (Strategy and strengths)
- Where are they vulnerable? (Weaknesses)
- Is the competitor content with their current positioning, or are they likely to change and possibly disrupt the market?

- What changes are they likely to make?
- How effective will these changes be?

BRANDING

A brand is a name, slogan, symbol, or design that is created to help identify a product, service, experience, or organization in the eyes of the consumer. It helps the consumer quickly to identify a product or service and its attributes. A brand has the ability to change consumer perceptions in ways that are not related to the actual characteristics of the product. It is thus a useful tool in promoting an organization and its products or services.

Your brand is the sum of your customer's perception of your products and services and their interaction with you – either directly or indirectly. Everything, from your organization's profile to how you present yourself on social media to your packaging, influences how people perceive your brand. Branding can be the difference between customers buying from you or buying from your competitors.

Once you have created your brand, you want to keep your customers loyal to it. The three most common factors that contribute to brand loyalty are:

- Customer satisfaction with the goods and services you provide.
- The customer's perception of the quality of your goods or services in terms of meeting their needs and wants.
- The customer's trust in the brand.

Professor Kevin Lane Keller[19] defined a brand equity model to help define a strong brand. The four steps of the model are:

1. Define Your Brand Identify: Who Are You?

You want to define your brand to stand out from your competitors. You then need to make sure your customers are aware of the brand and that they recognize it. You want it to be top of mind when they are thinking of your products or services. You want to create a clear association between the brand and your organization and its products or services. The image you want to portray through the brand needs to be apparent throughout all stages of customer interaction.

2. Brand Meaning: What Are You?

This is where you identify what your brand means and what it stands for. You then communicate this to your customers. There are two important building blocks to do this – *performance* and *imagery*.

Performance is how well your product or service meets the customer's functional needs, including its primary characteristics and features, product reliability, durability, serviceability, service effectiveness, efficiency, empathy, style and design, and price.

Imagery is about how well your brand meets your customer's social and psychological needs (values and meaning). You can increase brand imagery directly (experience with the brand) or indirectly (advertising or referral).

---

19   12manage Knowledge Centre, 2021, Brand Equity Model <https://www.12manage.com/description_keller_customer_based_brand_equity_model.html>,.

3. Brand Response: What Does The Customer Think And Feel About You?

Customers respond to your brand in two ways – by making *judgments* and by expressing their *feelings*.

Judgments are based on perceived and actual quality, credibility based on expertise (and innovation), trustworthiness, and likability.

Feelings are expressed about how your brand makes the customer feel. This could be directly about the brand or about how it makes them feel. Such feelings could include warmth, fun, excitement, security, social approval, and self-respect.

4. Brand Resonance: What About You And Me?

Your ultimate objective is for the consumer to want to have an ongoing relationship with your brand. This is the hardest of the four stages to achieve but is the most rewarding. To achieve brand resonance, you want your customers to:

- Be regular and repeat purchasers.
- Love your brand or product and see it as a special purchase.
- Feel a sense of community with the people associated with the brand.
- Engage actively with your brand through, for example, loyalty programs, forums, or marketing events.

5.3 Your Marketing Plan

AWARENESS

A marketing plan brings all the research and brainstorming together in one plan to define how you can serve your customers better in each segment.

The 7 Ps of Marketing is a tool to help define the various aspects of your marketing plan. The 7 Ps are product, price, promotion, place, people, process, and physical evidence. The 7 Ps digital equivalent are the 13 Cs of Digital Marketing.

ACTION

The following actions will help you to define your marketing plan:

- Determine where the opportunities are and how big they are. Where are the natural market extensions (geographic areas, new market segments)? How can you play a part in delivering these opportunities? What could your market share be? What does the future look like? What threats are there?

- Look at other markets (in other countries and in similar but different industries) to determine whether other successful methods could enhance your service offering.

- Can you service these new opportunities with your current operating model? How do you need to change your operating model to meet these opportunities? Do the opportunities outweigh the risks?

- Are there opportunities to acquire companies in target geographic areas or with relationships in target customer segments?

- What needs to be done to take advantage of the opportunities? What resources (suppliers, partners, networks, management, and staff) do you need to achieve success?

- Undertake a customer attitude survey to determine whether you are servicing their needs and where further opportunities exist to meet their needs.

- Review your customer base and ask where the opportunities are. Can you increase your focus on high-value or high-potential customers? Can you rationalize the customer portfolio? How can you improve the total customer experience?

- What quick improvements can you make that will improve your customers' experience and loyalty to your organization?

- Define a lead-generating system to take advantage of the opportunities identified. Ask yourself:

  - Where does your new business come from?

  - Do you have a system that generates enough new opportunities to meet your strategy?

  - How are you going to sell to your markets?

- Define a marketing plan for each market segment using the 7 Ps of Marketing or the 13 Cs of Digital Marketing. (See *THE 7 Ps OF MARKETING* and *THE 13 Cs OF DIGITAL MARKETING*)

THE 7 Ps OF MARKETING

The 7 Ps of Marketing is a tool to help you define the various aspects of your marketing strategy. Structure your marketing plans around each of the 7 Ps. Remember that the 7 Ps model is not all-encompassing – you will need to consider other factors that might be relevant to your organization.

PRODUCT

Product refers to what you are selling, including all the features, advantages, and benefits that your customers can enjoy from buying your goods or services. Product encompasses quality, image, branding, features, variants, mix, support, customer service, use occasion, availability, and warranties. Ask yourself:

- What do your customers need?
- Do your current products or services (or your mix of products and services) meet your customers' needs?
- Is your product or service superior to that of your competitors? Where are you superior? Could you develop an area of superiority?
- What substitutes do your customers buy? What can I learn from them? How can I change my service offering?
- How can you develop your products or services to improve your offering in the eyes of your customers? How can you improve your standards?
- Are you making the most of the products and services you already offer? How can you change your product or service appeal?
- What products or services should you abandon?

PRICE

Price refers to your pricing strategy for your products and services and how it will affect your customers. It includes list prices, discounts, credit, payment methods, and free or value-added elements. Ask yourself:

- Are your products and services correctly priced for your customer base? How much are your customers prepared to pay? What other pricing options do they want?

- Do you enjoy high margins? Do you cover your overheads and costs? Can you improve your margins where you have tailored your service offering to meet your customer's needs? Can you coordinate the pricing of complementary products and services?

- How do your prices compare to those of competitors? What can you learn from this?

- How can you change your pricing model?

PROMOTION

These are promotional activities you use to make your customers aware of your products and services, such as advertising, sales tactics, promotions, and direct marketing. Promotion can be achieved through marketing communications, personal promotion, sales promotion, public relations, branding, and direct marketing. Ask yourself:

- Are your promotional activities continuously increasing your sales?

- How do your competitors promote their products successfully?

- How can you add to or substitute these promotional activities?
- Are you utilizing the most effective sales and advertising channels?

PLACE

Place is where your products and services are seen, made, sold, or distributed, including segmented trade channels and sales support. Ask yourself:

- Where do your customers want to buy from you? How do they go about buying?
- How do your customers find you?
- What channels do your competitors use?
- What impact are disruptive technologies making on the sales process? Are there new distribution options?
- In what additional markets could you offer your products or services?
- In what way should you change your distribution channels?

PEOPLE

People refers to the staff and salespeople who work for your organization, including yourself. It includes those working on marketing activities and initiatives, people who are in contact with your customers, recruitment methods, culture, image, training and skills, and remuneration. Ask yourself:

- Do you have the right people servicing your customers? Where are the skills gaps?
- What can you do to improve your customer service team? For example, hiring new people, repositioning existing

people, providing ongoing training, and letting go of underperformers.

- Can you improve the understanding of price margins with your sales staff?

- Does your reward system promote the behavior you require from your sales staff? Can you build sales profitability into sales incentives?

PROCESS

These are the processes involved in delivering your products and services to the customer and include customer focus, technology support, design features, and research and development. Ask yourself:

- How easy is it to do business with you?

- How consistent are your customers' sales experiences?

- What impression do you want to create with your customers? What would you have to do in every customer interaction to create the ideal impression? What changes do you want to make in the way you interact with customers to become a preferred supplier?

PHYSICAL EVIDENCE

Physical evidence is everything your customers see when interacting with your organization. It includes product packaging, support, the organization's look and feel (buildings, vehicles, staff, documentation, and electronic media), and customer contact experience. Ask yourself:

- Do you have a clearly defined image aligned to your strategy?

- Do your customers perceive you as you want them to?

- How can you reassure your customers through your image? For example, you might want to focus on upgrading your physical environment, your packaging, your branding, and your website, or making sure that your staff is well trained and presentable and that your vehicles are always clean.

- How consistently is your image applied across your entire organization?

- Does your image create new opportunities for you?

The 7 Ps are continually evolving and are by no means limited to seven. Suggested additions include:

- *Planet*: to cater for growing environmental awareness and good stewardship of the environment;

- *Privacy*: covering the risks of sharing consumer data; and

- *Poverty:* opening up new markets previously not considered because of the low incomes of the potential customers.

13 Cs OF DIGITAL MARKETING

The 13 Cs are the equivalent of the 7 Ps but in the digital world. The factors making up the 7 Ps, while valid, need to be adapted to meet digital requirements. These points are focused on your digital selling platform as opposed to general information that you might have on a website.

CUSTOMER

You want to understand your target customers. Your customers and their needs are continually changing. Do you know their needs and how they are changing? Do you know their favorite media channels? How do they find you?

You need to be where your customers are digitally and need to project your offering in a manner that appeals to them.

CHANNEL

What is the ideal marketing channel for you to use? Your target audience is searching for solutions to their problems, so your solution must meet their needs.

Your core digital presence should always be your website. Its focus should be driven by your target audience and how you want to interact with them. If you want to sell, then design your website around the customers' experience and entice them to buy. Make sure your website encourages the closing of the deal. If your website is primarily aimed at informing and interacting with stakeholders (like investors), then your focus will be to meet their needs.

What if you have multiple needs you need to meet? Look for innovative ways of meeting multiple needs without compromising any one of your stakeholder groupings. For example, use multiple websites or apps directing each particular stakeholder group to where you want them to be.

Once you have perfected your website, look at other forms of digital media to improve the way you interact with your customers and entice them to visit your retail platform. While you always want to be where your customers are, be aware of trends in social media usage. Some questions to ask yourself include:

- Which social media platforms are growing and which are declining?

- Are you prepared to continue using a social media platform that you believe might compromise your brand?

CREATIVITY

You want to find creative ways to capture your target's attention by developing new and innovative ways to inform, educate and persuade your customers to buy from you. Competition is fierce, and you want to ensure that you come out tops.

Update your website regularly, not only to remain relevant but to take advantage of search engine optimization. Google ranks websites that update their content regularly higher than websites that don't.

You might not be able to afford to be the market leader, but make sure you are not the laggard. Laggards tend to die. Review your offering continually to ensure that you are among the leaders.

CONSISTENCY

Make sure your message is consistent across all channels, be it your website, across your social media, your emails, or in your advertising. Inconsistency can cause confusion. Confusion leads to a loss of confidence. Customers who lack confidence in your offering will look elsewhere.

Make sure your target market continually sees value in your offering.

CREDIBILITY

Credibility is key in digital markets. Your customers are interacting with a digital representation of your organization, and they need to trust that what they see is what they will get. Enhance your credibility by allowing customers to review their experience or purchases, and offer hassle-free returns and money-back policies.

CONNECTION

When making initial contact with a potential customer, how do you stay in touch? No one likes in-your-face marketing messages or being marketed at – people generally prefer being *communicated with*. Your strategy is to inform, educate and persuade your target market in a way that they understand and in a way that creates trust.

There are multiple means of communicating with customers. The proliferation of communication platforms and social media has created two-way – and even multi-party – dialogue opportunities, often resulting in a loss of control by organizations. The speed of response to messages, questions, or comments on these different platforms is critical to retaining some control, especially when it comes to limiting negative publicity.

When looking to reach a broader audience than you currently serve through your digital presence, remember that you need to ensure that your marketing message has a broad cultural feel. Don't assume your culture applies to the world.

CONVENIENCE

The digital economy has helped to drive the need for immediate satisfaction. Your organization should be able to offer your services across multiple devices. Access needs to be quick and from anywhere. There must be an easy recall of past orders to allow for repeat purchases. You need to have simple mechanisms in place for order acknowledgments and follow-ups.

CUSTOMIZATION

Use data to optimize the customer experience but don't overdo it – you don't want to look like a stalker! Ask your customers to help with product design in the ideation stage. Customize and personalize products. Consider rewarding regular customers, including offering different pricing strategies for bulk or frequent purchases, as well as location or other discounts.

COORDINATION

Make sure you can deliver what you promise. You cannot afford to allow a fantastic shopping experience to be let down by poor delivery – nothing destroys trust faster. Continually test the delivery process and make sure it lives up to the shopping experience.

CUSTOMER SERVICE

Your first customer service point should be digital. Make sure a customer can answer the majority of their queries easily through an easy-to-use query section. When there are problems, make sure these are answered quickly and comprehensively.

COMPETITION

Continually review what your competition is doing and the strategies they employ. Are your prices competitive? Look out for game-changing technologies.

CHANGE

Adjust your marketing strategy continually to cater to changing customer needs, changing societal dynamics, and changing technology.

COST-EFFECTIVE

Is developing your digital presence and marketing your organization cost-effective? Don't spend a fortune on developing a solution that could be done as effectively for significantly less. Target your advertising and monitor the results. Continually tinker with your formula to maximize your return.

5.4 Innovating your Products and Services

AWARENESS

Markets continue to change and splinter, making it necessary to develop an innovation strategy that allows the organization to adapt quickly to meet changing demands. Speed in meeting these changes provides a competitive edge. Aim to make your top products or services obsolete before your competitors do.

Every product or service needs to be:

- *Desirable*: ask yourself – do people want it?
- *Feasible*: ask yourself – can you deliver to meet your customer's needs?
- *Viable*: ask yourself – can you earn a profit?

Even if one of these three is missing, your product or service will, in all likelihood, not be successful.

ACTION

The following actions will help you to innovate your products and services.

- Review your portfolio of products and services. (See *PRODUCT OR SERVICE REVIEW*)

- Take a slumbering product or service and meet with employees, customers, suppliers, and distributors to brainstorm relaunching it. Devise a low-investment strategy to differentiate the product or service radically through value-adding steps. Relaunch the product or service within six months.

- You will need champions to drive new product development. When appointing a champion, focus on their passion. Cheer them on and support them, especially when a project fails.

- Use multi-functional teams to develop new or enhanced products and services. Involve your suppliers, distributors, and customers. Reward team successes. (See *INNOVATION CYCLE*)

- Replace proposals for new ideas with pilots or prototypes. Develop trial sites to test new products. Keep looking for pilot opportunities. Aim to reduce your development time.

- Challenge employees to come up with the most implementable idea.

- Look at what you can learn from competitors and interesting non-competitors without necessarily reinventing their products or services yourself.

- Organize new product marketing efforts around word-of-mouth or social networking.

- Make sure you encourage innovation. End inertia, take action, and destroy barriers. Look for quick modifications, but don't reinvent the wheel. Recognize innovation, no matter how small or simple.

- There will be more failures as you move quickly into developing new ideas. Failed efforts that are well thought out, executed with speed, quickly adjusted, and learned from should be rewarded – this is the type of action you want.

- Measure innovation – what gets measured gets done. You want to recognize improvements to customer satisfaction. Remember that customers are more likely to recognize small improvements than you are.

- Innovation becomes a way of life. Continuous change is imperative. Assess every action in light of its contribution to an increased capacity for change.

PRODUCT OR SERVICE REVIEW

Review your current product or service portfolio. (See *SCAMPER*)

The questions below will help you in your review:

1. How well has your product or service been adopted by your customers? (See *MEASURING ADOPTION*)

2. Can you improve your focus on the most profitable products and services?

3. Can you broaden your product and service features, functionality, and value?

4. Can you rationalize or refocus your products and services?

5. Can you use current product and service components to open new opportunities?

6. Can you use your branding on unbranded products?

7. Is there an opportunity to license or acquire products and intellectual property?

8. Are there opportunities to tailor products and services to meet the requirements of new customer segments?

9. Can technology be used to enhance current products or services?

10. What is the threat of technology development to current product or service offering?

11. Are there opportunities to improve the quality and reliability of products and services?

12. Can you shorten the order-to-delivery cycle time or improve product and service availability?

13. Can you design your products for materials efficiency or scalability?

14. Can you increase the number and quality of product or service launches?

15. Are there opportunities to acquire companies with aligned product or service strategies?

16. Can you improve upon design and development processes?

17. Can you improve upon collaboration with design, development, and production partners?

18. Are there R&D tax and economic development incentives of which you can take advantage?

19. Can you reduce the need for routine after-sales support?

20. Can you convert free services into money-generating opportunities?

21. Can you improve your product or packaging for easier distribution or be more environmentally friendly?

22. Are your products correctly priced? Are you making profits on all your products and services? (See *ACTIVITY-BASED COSTING*)

Adapted from: Tom Peters' *Thriving on Chaos*

INNOVATION CYCLE

Stanford University's d.school developed the following innovation process:

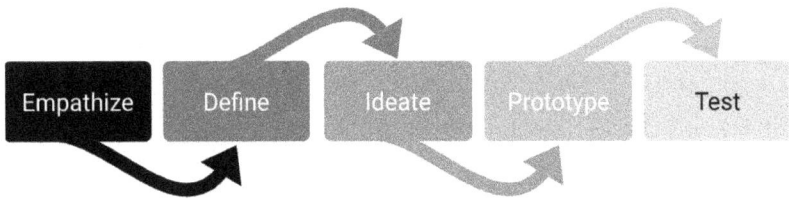

d.school's Innovation Cycle

- **Empathize** with your target customer. If your target market is a child, try to think like that child and see the need from their eyes. Empathy for your target customer is a critical first step. Understand their needs and build your product or experience to meet their needs.

- **Define** – you have understood the customer's need by empathizing with their situation. Now define an actionable problem statement to help you focus on solving their need.

- **Ideate** – generate as many ideas as possible to solve the problem. Choose the best option.

- **Prototype** – build the chosen solution. The prototype does not have to be fancy; its purpose is to validate and test the solution.

- **Test** – take your prototype to your target customers and get their reaction to your proposed product. What worked? What did not? What have you learned? Take these learnings and go back to Ideate, Prototype, and Test.

Adapted from Jason Barron's *The Visual MBA: A Quick Guide to Everything You'll Learn in Two Years of Business School.*

SCAMPER

The SCAMPER checklist was developed by educational expert Bob Eberle and will help you to review your products or services. Run through your products or services asking the following SCAMPER questions:

- *Substitute*: What can you substitute? (People, components, material)

- *Combine*: What can you combine with other products or services?

- *Adapt*: What can you adapt to improve? (Function, appearance)

- *Modify*: Can you modify the size, shape, texture, sound (and so on)?

- *Put to other use*: What other uses are there for the product or service?

- *Eliminate*: What can you eliminate, reduce or simplify?

- *Reverse*: Can you "reverse" the product or service to create something different?

Adapted from Mikael Krogerus and Roman Tschäppelar's *The Decision Book – Fifty Models for Strategic Thinking*.

MEASURING ADOPTION

Adopting a product or service requires a balance of price, benefit, ease of use, and ease of purchase. If your product or service has strengths in all four of these areas, the adoption by customers will be greater.

To undertake this exercise, take each of your products or services and score them on a scale of 1 to 5 (1 being poor and 5 being great) against each of the criteria relative to its competitors (balance of price, benefit, ease of use, and ease of purchase). Map your scores using a Radar Chart, as depicted below:

Low pricing

5
4
3
2
1
0

◇ Product A
◇ Product B
◇ Product C
◇ Product D

Easy to purchase

Superior benefits

Ease of use

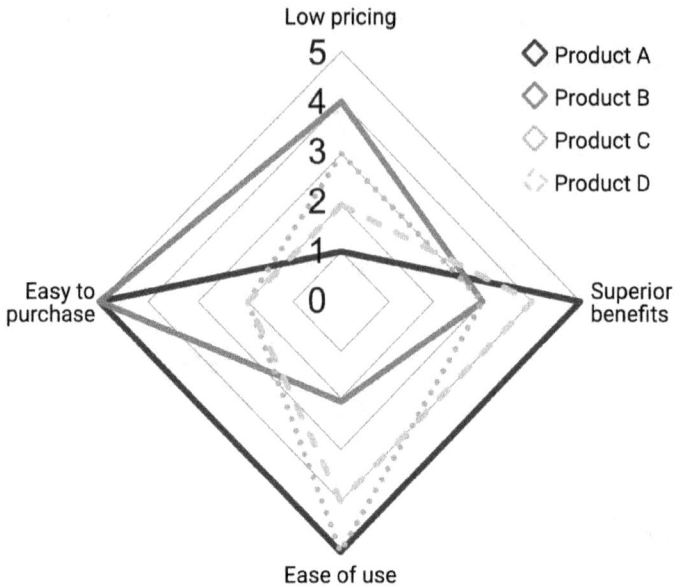

Product Adoption

Each product aims to move its score outwards. In the above example, Product A is expensive relative to competitor products but ranks well in all other areas. Product A's price needs to be reduced to increase its adoption and market penetration. Product B needs to be easier to use and has average benefits. Product C is easy to use but falls short in all other dimensions. Product D needs work both on price and ease of purchase.

Adapted from Jason Barron's *The Visual MBA: A Quick Guide to Everything You'll Learn in Two Years of Business School.*

ACTIVITY-BASED COSTING

Activity-based costing (ABC) is a process of allocating indirect costs to, for example, products or services, customers, or channels, based on the activity that generates the cost. Traditional cost accounting models allocate indirect costs based on specific criteria, such as volume. Thus, high-volume items tend to carry a greater cost burden than low-volume items.

ABC helps by giving a more accurate (or truer) cost for customers, services, or products. You can use ABC to:

- Determine your profitable customer, channels, products, services, or divisions.
- Determine break-even prices for products and services.
- Identify areas for improvement.

The following steps will help you to undertake an ABC exercise. To illustrate ABC in practice, let's consider this example of a company that manufactures wooden chairs and tables.

Step 1: Identify the indirect activities that are required (or necessary) to complete the product or deliver the service

In this example, the primary activities might be materials handling and manufacturing set-up. All other activities are assumed to be too difficult to differentiate and are grouped as "other."

Step 2: Assign overhead costs to the indirect activities identified in Step 1

In our example, the assumption is total overheads of $1 000 000, of which $210 000 can be allocated to materials handling and $100 000 to machine set-up. The unallocated $690 000 makes up the "other" overheads.

Step 3: Determine the cost driver behind each activity identified in Step 1

A cost driver is the unit of an activity that causes the change in the activity's cost. In our example, the cost drivers are assumed to be:

- Materials handling: cubic meters of timber consumed (700 m^3 for the year).

- Machine set-up: number of times machines are set up per annum (50 times in a year).

- Other overheads: running machine time (10 000 hours per year).

Step 4: Determine the overhead costs per activity

The overhead costs per unit of cost driver per activity are:

Activity	Cost driver	Overhead	Units	Cost per unit
Materials handling	m³ of timber	$210 000	700	$300/m³
Machine set-up	Number of set-ups p.a.	$100 000	50	$2 000/set-up
Other overheads	Machine hours	$690 000	10 000	$69/hour

Step 5: Determine direct costs

The direct costs could include materials used, labor, and consumables. In our example, we have assumed the following direct costs per unit manufactured to be as follows:

Direct costs	Chair	Table
Materials	$50	$75
Labor	$100	$50
Consumables	$10	$15
Total per unit	**$160**	**$140**

Step 6: Cost the product

In our example, we assume annual sales volumes of tables to be 2 000, with chairs at 12 000 for the year. Chairs would account for 467 m³ of wood and 25 set-ups. Tables would account for 233 m³ of wood and 25 set-ups. Machine time would be 0.556 hours per chair and 1.667 hours per table.

The costs per table and chair are:

Costs	Chair		Table	
	Overhead costs			
Materials handling	(467x$300)	$140 100	(233x$300)	$69 900
Machine set-up	(25x$2000)	$50 000	(25x$2000)	$50 000
Other overheads	(0.556x12000x$69)	$460 368	(1.667x2000x$69)	$230 046
	Direct costs			
Materials	(12000x$50)	$600 000	(2000x$75)	$150 000
Labor	(12000x$100)	$1 200 000	(2000x$150)	$100 000
Consumables	(12000x$10)	$120 000	(2000x$15)	$30 000
	Total costs			
Total costs		$2 570 468		$629 946
Cost per unit		$214.21		$314.97

Step 7: Analysis

By using ABC, you can determine a more realistic cost – and, therefore, the profitability of your products – when compared to other costing methods. From the analysis, you can decide where you need to increase prices, reduce costs, or even discontinue lines.

The analysis can also be used to examine various scenarios. In the example, you can determine how reducing the number of set-ups (by having longer batch runs) will impact costs. When doing such an analysis, all factors need to be taken into consideration before making any final decisions. In our example, increasing batch runs would mean carrying a larger inventory of finished goods, with the associated costs of carrying inventory.

6

Increasing Sales

Selling is about building on your marketing strategy by putting your marketing plans into action.

Your sales process starts with a sales strategy defining how you are going to get your products or services in front of your customer. Your sales strategy is the operating plan for your sales force, allowing you to manage your sales workforce and resources better.

Sales Strategy

Your sales strategy includes:

- Your sales message and approach to customer engagement, including a behavioral blueprint for your sales force.

- Your sales process when acquiring new customers, developing opportunities, managing your pipeline, and integrating into customer relations management (CRM). (See *A TYPICAL SALES PROCESS*)

- How you intend to manage your sales function (managers and workforce), including best practices, coaching, and metrics.

- Your ideal sales competencies and behavior, as well as a gap analysis between ideal and actual, which will be used to define your sales force skills development plan. The plan would include how you propose to recruit the right people with strengths aligned to your sales objectives, your approach to rewarding them, and plans to execute your strategy – including the ongoing development of your entire sales team.

How to sell is currently beyond the scope of this tool.

In this module, we look at growing sales from existing clients through partnering and developing your sales network as approaches to improving your sales.

A TYPICAL SALES PROCESS

The following is a typical seven-step sales process:

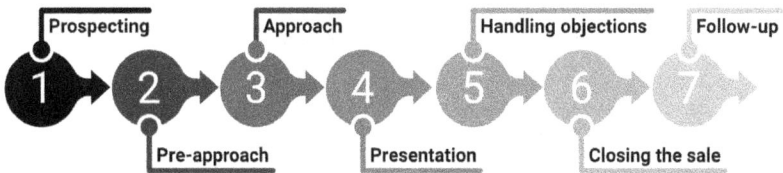

A Typical Sales Process

- **Prospecting** involves searching for and qualifying new customers who have needs that the organization's products or services can meet. Qualifying consists of ensuring that the potential customer has a need, can afford the services, and has the authority to make a decision. This is normally a data collation step, and the potential customer is not contacted.

- The **Pre-approach** step involves preparing to approach the customer. Further information is collected on the potential customer and their needs, and the sales approach is finalized.

- The **Approach** step is the first interaction with the customer. The objective is to gain the attention of the customer and to build an initial rapport. There are several ways of achieving this, including product giveaways, referrals, asking questions, demonstrating the benefits of the products or services, and offering advice.

- The **Presentation** step involves making the pitch to the customer. Before this happens, make sure you are familiar with the customer and their needs. Your focus is to move the customer from being aware of your products or services to considering buying from you.

- The **Handling Objections** step consists of answering the customer's queries or dealing with their hesitations.

- **Closing the Sale** involves taking the order and completing any final negotiations, for example, payment terms and delivery options.

- The **Follow-up step** is about retaining what is needed for future sales, primarily through ensuring customer satisfaction.

6.1 Partnering With Your Customer

AWARENESS

The most cost-effective marketing option with a small marketing budget is to develop a customer-driven strategy. The better the quality of your relationship with your customer, the more business they will give you. The exception to this rule is where you have a unique product that is not available elsewhere.

People like to deal with people who are similar to themselves. Establish rapport by becoming like the person you are doing business with. Mirror your customer's behavior. Build rapport, and you will build sales.

Building partnerships with customers goes beyond just relationships. Aim to know their business better than they do. Understand their needs. Find out how you can add value to their business.

You can add value by:

- Providing valuable perspectives on your customer's markets.
- Educating your customer on new issues or outcomes.
- Advising your customer on the issues they face.
- Helping the customer by presenting them with the different alternatives available to them.
- Being a supplier that is easy to buy from.

This approach follows three steps:

1. Start a relationship and aim to be invited back.

2. Maintain the relationship and get to know your customer's business better than they do.

3. Create a partnership by getting to know your customer's customer so that you can add value to their business.

Adapted from David Hall and Dinah Bennett's *The Hallmarks for Successful Business.*

ACTION

The following actions will help to improve partnering with your customer:

- Choose a selection of up to twenty customers that can drive the success of your organization.

- Get to understand their businesses and their most pressing needs. Spend time at their business. Find out how they use your product or service. Ask why they use it that way. Find out who their customers are. Determine how you can help them help their customers.

- Get to know the needs of *their* customers – needs that *they* can solve. Determine how you can help your customer solve their customers' needs.

- Match your differentiators to each customer's needs. Do this by listing your differentiators and the outcomes that your customer most cares about. Ask:

  - Which of your differentiators does your customer undervalue?

  - What customer needs do you not fully help to resolve? Can you address these needs?

  - Review the outcomes and determine how to serve the customer best in the future.

- Give them exactly what they want, and do it better than anyone else. Deliver on your promises.

- Keep in regular contact with your customers and not just when you want an order from them. Treat them as individuals. Show respect for their time, views, and opinions – and their business. Deal with them in a friendly but professional manner.

- Consider using a customer relationship management (CRM) package to help manage your customers. (See *WHAT MAKES A GOOD CRM SYSTEM*)

WHAT MAKES A GOOD CRM SYSTEM

When looking for a CRM software solution, consider the following:

1. It must enable your salespeople. Unless they can see the benefit to themselves, they won't use it.

2. It must make your salespeople more effective, not just more efficient.

3. It must enable communication between team members.

4. It must integrate with your other systems (for example, emails, calendars), sync with the different hardware (phones, laptops, tablets), and operate on the different mobile operating systems (for example, iOS, Android) that your salespeople use.

5. The reporting functionality must cover more than just sales and the sales pipeline. You want it to provide all the reports related to your sales function.

6. It must be simple to use and quick to set up.

7. Make sure that technical support is included in the package and is not an add-on.

8. The system must be cost-effective relative to your organization's profitability.

6.2 Your Sales Network

AWARENESS

Finding customers is always a challenge. Opportunities have been opened up to organizations through social and other media, such as Facebook and Google. Even with the advent of new technologies, networking is still a significant tool for companies to use. Networking covers developing and maintaining relationships with people who can impact your organization directly or indirectly. Networks are intended to be mutually beneficial, extending the concept of teamwork beyond your immediate peer group.

The type of network changes across the sales cycle. The sales cycle of identifying a prospect, gaining buy-in, creating solutions, and closing the deal is used to discuss the various types of networks needed for successful sales.

The network groupings, as defined by Tuba Üstüner and David Godes in their Harvard Business Review article entitled *Better Sales Networks*,[20] are:

---

20   Tuba Üstüner and David Godes, Better Sales Networks, Harvard Business Review, <https://hbr.org/2006/07/better-sales-networks>.

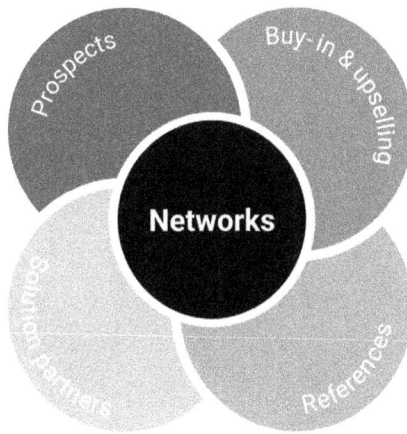

Üstüner's Network Groupings

When identifying *prospects*, you want a network as broad as possible that will provide you with timely information on opportunities and market developments. You want to know about leads on opportunities before they become public knowledge. Such a person might not be obvious. Look at the type of lead you want and ask yourself who is likely to know about a possible opportunity long before it gets to the request-for-proposal stage. Think out of the box. For example, would a realtor selling a house to an out-of-town business person be an indicator of opportunities?

Gaining *buy-in and upselling* is all about gaining an understanding of your customer's problems, which you are going to help solve by introducing them to your product or service. Here you are looking at identifying decision-makers and influencers. You want to develop stronger ties within a customer's organization. It would help if you mapped out the prospect organization's internal network and how it works. You are looking for who makes the decisions, who influences the decisions, who has formal authority, who has informal authority, how decisions are made, who has access to information, and finally, who the one person is who knows everything that is going on within the organization to point you in the right direction.

Creating *solutions* to customer problems is often a team effort. With large organizations, it is about developing an internal organizational network and asking who would be willing to work with you to help develop the solution? With smaller companies, you might want to create a network of organizations that will help you develop the solution. Such a network will be based on the ability of your network to deliver to the standard you want for customer commitment.

The final network grouping is *references*. Customers are influenced by past customers' experiences. You need to find current customers that are willing to act as references. A word of warning – don't overuse any one reference.

ACTION

The following actions will help to improve your sales networking:

- List your current networks and then divide them into the four categories as per the sales cycle:
  - Prospect Generation Network
  - Customer Network (for both potential and existing customers)
  - Solution or Marketplace Network
  - Reference Site Network
- Describe how they add to your network or their role.
- Score every member of your network with either a plus (+), a minus (–), or an equals sign (=):

- + if they add value to your organization.
- – if they detract from the organization's value.
- = if they are neutral.

- Use the plusses to build your organization. Decide how to convert the negatives or neutrals to become positives.

- Identify those in your network that you want to contact more frequently. Utilize a diary to manage this.

- Review your networks and identify gaps. Determine actions to grow these networks. Remember to use your network to help you grow your network – it really works!

- Service your network – it is a two-way process. How can you give back to the people who have helped you? For example, you might want to send them market information, job opportunities, ideas, or leads.

- Start a network file on each of your network members. Look for software – like a CRM package – to help you manage your networks.

- If you have salespeople working for you, devise a means of keeping tabs on their networks so that you don't lose the network when the salesperson leaves you.

7

Operations

This chapter is about delivery through operations. Four main aspects are discussed:

- Your Value Chain: Operations can be defined using a value chain. A value chain describes the process by which an organization delivers value to its customers to realize a profit. The purpose of this module is to review your organization's value chain and determine what needs to change to ensure the delivery of the vision.

- Resources to Deliver: Resources are scarce. This module covers optimizing the allocation of limited resources across the value chain to deliver the vision.

- Your Delivery Partners: Your delivery partners are those entities independent of your organization that you partner with to satisfy your customer's needs. You cannot deliver your products or services without these delivery partners.

The focus of this module is to identify your key delivery partners and determine strategies to optimize your relationships with these partners.

- Your Structure: Your organization's structure is a system that outlines how your value chain activities are to be directed to achieve the vision. Structure should only be considered after reviewing your value chain, resources, and delivery partners.

7.1 Your Value Chain

AWARENESS

The delivery of goods and services to the customer takes place through a combination of formal and informal processes and tasks. At the highest level, there are *activities*. Each activity has inputs (for example, raw materials into operations) and outputs (for example, finished goods from operations). Outputs from one activity are the inputs to the next activity. Combining these activities results in meeting the customer's needs, which results in margins and ultimately profits.

Collectively, these activities make up the organization's value chain. Michael Porter[21] defined the concept of a value chain model. The value chain model consists of two core groupings of activities, namely, primary and support activities, as depicted in the diagram below:

---

21   Michael E Porter. Competitive Advantage. Free Press, 1985.

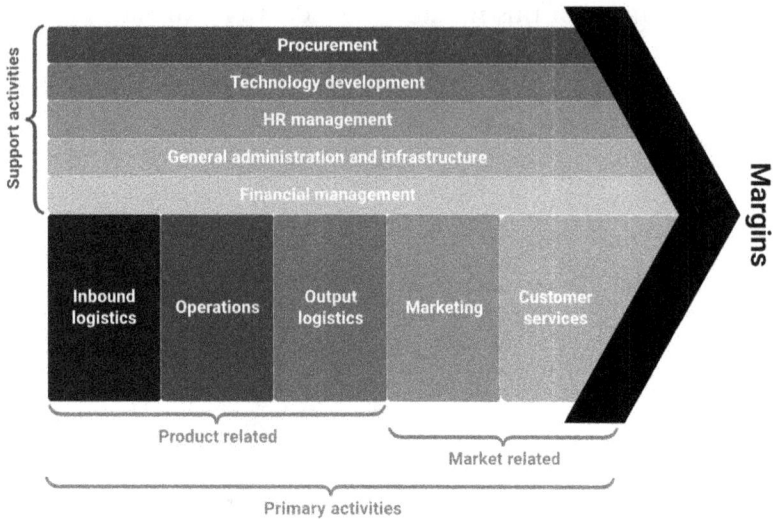

Porter's Value Chain

Primary activities are split into two categories – product-related and market-related. The primary activities typically consist of:

- Inbound logistics: including receiving, handling, warehousing, and distributing inputs, such as raw materials (Product).

- Operations: transforming inputs into the final product or output (Product).

- Output logistics: distribution of the product to customers (Product).

- Marketing: persuading customers to buy (Market).

- Customer services: maintaining the value of the product during and after the sales process (Market).

Support activities typically include:

- Procurement (primarily of inputs)

- Technology development

- Human resource management

- General administration and infrastructure

- Financial management

These definitions are academic and may not mean much to you or your organization. You need to define your value chain based on how you deliver solutions to your customers. The diagram below takes the same information and presents it in a different format and includes additional information. The primary activities are shown as process flows at the top of the diagram. Each prime activity has a number of sub-activities that are listed below each primary activity. Support activities are listed at the bottom of the diagram.

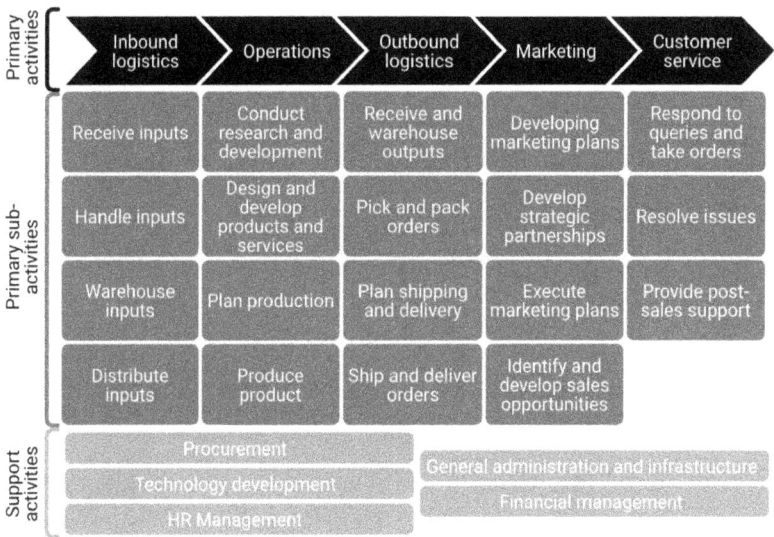

Primary activities	Inbound logistics	Operations	Outbound logistics	Marketing	Customer service
Primary sub-activities	Receive inputs	Conduct research and development	Receive and warehouse outputs	Developing marketing plans	Respond to queries and take orders
	Handle inputs	Design and develop products and services	Pick and pack orders	Develop strategic partnerships	Resolve issues
	Warehouse inputs	Plan production	Plan shipping and delivery	Execute marketing plans	Provide post-sales support
	Distribute inputs	Produce product	Ship and deliver orders	Identify and develop sales opportunities	
Support activities	Procurement				
	Technology development		General administration and infrastructure		
	HR Management		Financial management		

An Alternate Value Chain

The purpose of defining your value chain is to understand how value is delivered and to identify what needs to change to optimize delivery of your vision. With the value chain, there is no one-size-fits-all answer for every organization. There is only what you and your management team feel is the best way to deliver solutions to your customers.

ACTION

The following actions will help you to define your value chain:

- Start by defining your current value chain. Define your current high-level business activities. What are the primary activities you follow to deliver products and services to your customers? Define them from a logical process flow point of view. Is there a clearly defined input and output for each activity? Each output from one activity should be the input to the next activity.

- Define your primary sub-activities or processes and add them to your diagram. You are aiming at high-level processes, so don't go into too much detail. Detailed process design is covered in a later chapter.

- Define your current support activities.

- Document your deliberations into a value chain model. This will be your current value chain. You might want to follow one of the examples provided above, or you might want to define your own model. Don't be limited by the examples shown. Capture as much information as you see necessary to define your value chain. You might need to go to the next level of detail before you can fully define your value chain.

- Review your current value chain, asking: How can you improve performance and customer delivery? How can you ensure better connectivity with the various internal and external stakeholders? How can you improve the integration of processes? Will the value chain help in growing and scaling the organization quickly? Will risk management be improved? What support activities are necessary to ensure the delivery of the primary activities? (See *PRIMARY ACTIVITIES* and *SUPPORT ACTIVITIES*)

- Revise your value chain to define how you would like your organization to operate. This then becomes your target value chain.

- Review your current value chain against your target value chain. Where are there differences between the two models? What needs to change? What can you let go of?

- Define projects that are necessary to implement your target value chain. Estimate the costs of these projects, not just in monetary value but also in terms of factors like timing, people costs, and impacts, to decide which projects are worth investing in. Prioritize these projects, looking for affordable projects that will make a difference in as short a time as possible.

- Determine a plan to implement the target value chain, including the order of implementation.

- Review your strategy to determine whether you need to change anything as a result of your target value chain implementation plan.

PRIMARY ACTIVITIES

The questions posed below are there to prod your thought process when reviewing your value chain. Some of the questions might not apply to your organization, but don't discard them too quickly. Rather ask yourself if the question, rephrased, would be applicable elsewhere. Similarly, there may be some parts of your organization that are not covered by these questions. Examine these areas in light of the spirit of these questions to determine your ideal value chain.

INBOUND LOGISTICS

Inbound logistics includes the receiving, handling, storing, and internal distribution of raw materials (or basic ingredients) of a product or service.

The following questions will help you in your review of this area:

- How do you forecast demand? Can this be improved on?
- What product/inventory/raw material do you use in production or other processes? Is there an alternative product that is cheaper/better/has less environmental impact?
- What inventory levels do you want to hold? What are the forecast demand levels? What are the lead times to replenish inventory levels?
- How do you control and check your inventory? Do you need inventory/warehousing management software?
- Do you have the necessary space and equipment to warehouse and handle your inventory?
- What are you going to do with obsolete, slow-moving, or damaged items?
- Can technology be used to enhance the function?
- How can you improve communications, both internally and externally?

- How can you improve your workforce's output and efficiencies?

OPERATIONS

Operations involve the transforming of inputs into the final product or service.

The following questions will help you in your review of this area:

- Are the plant, facilities, and equipment suitable and safe in terms of correct design, construction, and maintenance?

- Do you have a formal quality assurance program covering the entire spectrum from raw materials at the supplier to a final product in the customer's warehouse?

- Do you have documented Standard Operating Procedures (SOP) covering who does what, when, and how? Does the SOP cover the entire flow from raw materials at the supplier's plant to delivery to the customer?

- Do you have verifiable records of all operations?

- How can you improve your processes? How can you utilize technology to improve them?

- Can you (or should you) outsource elements of your operations? Can you insource functions that are currently outsourced?

- Do you have a production plan showing costs and volumes?

- How can you improve communications, both internally and externally?

- How can you improve your workforce's output and efficiencies?

OUTPUT LOGISTICS

Output logistics consists of the delivery of products and services to the customer. These include storage, distribution (systems), and transport.

The following questions will help you in your review of this area:

- What inventory levels do you want to hold (fixed stock levels or just-in-time)? What are the forecast demand levels? What are the lead times to replenish inventory levels?

- How do you control and check your inventory? Do you need inventory/warehousing management software?

- Do you have the necessary space and equipment to warehouse and handle your inventory?

- What do you plan to do with obsolete, slow-moving, or damaged items?

- How do you distribute inventory to customers or outlets? Is there a more efficient/cost-effective/environmentally friendly way to do this?

- Do you use distribution or delivery partners? Are they strategic partners? Can you find better partners?

- Can you use technology to improve this function?

- How can you improve communications, both internally and externally?

- How can you improve your workforce's output and efficiencies?

MARKETING

Marketing is the process of setting oneself apart from one's competitors and creating advantages for the customer, thus persuading them to buy.

The following questions will help you in your review of this area:

- Have you defined your customer groupings, and know their needs?
- Have you differentiated your products and services to meet the needs of your customers?
- How can you improve your market penetration?
- Do you have a marketing plan defining how you service each of your customer groupings?
- How can you improve on or replace your products and services?
- Can technology be used to enhance your processes?
- How can you improve communications, both internally and externally?
- How can you improve the output and efficiencies of your workforce?

CUSTOMER SERVICE

Customer service is the maintenance of the value of the product or service during the sales process and thereafter.

The following questions will help you in your review of this area:

- How can you improve your customer's experience when dealing with your organization?

- How do you partner with your customers? How can you improve on this?

- How do you attract new customers? Can you improve on this?

- Do you monitor your sales trends? How can you be more responsive to movements in these trends?

- What can you do to improve your margins?

- Can technology be used to enhance your processes?

- How can you improve communications, both internally and externally?

- How can you improve the output and efficiencies of your workforce?

SUPPORT ACTIVITIES

The support functions covered are procurement, information technology (IT), human resources (HR), and finance. Different organizations will have other support functions specific to them. The primary purpose of any support function must be to support the organization in achieving its vision.

Support functions are often "grudge" purchases in that they take up limited resources but don't always appear to add value to the organization's operations. But, when established and managed correctly, support functions add *enormous* value to an organization. To add value, they need to offer specialist skills and services that add value to line functions (those delivering the primary activities). These services need to be aligned with the strategy of the organization. Openness and transparency about what each support function does and how it adds value are imperative. Support functions should be proactive in determining the services required by the line functions.

A new support function is often established to meet a need, particularly where an in-house function is more cost-effective than outsourcing. Such needs could include doing administrative or regulatory tasks, or providing specialist services. A newly established support function is typically manned by inexperienced people and lacks resources. For example, the finance function might start with a bookkeeper keeping financial records. An external accountant might assist with the set-up of the financial systems and policies. When establishing a new function, limit the mandate to ensure good delivery in that particular area. The scope of the function can be expanded once expertise is gained. Similarly, start with a small team, hire the best specialist you can afford, and grow the team from there.

As a support function becomes successful, they will typically want to grow the role they play in an organization. Uncontrolled growth can be problematic. The growth of services offered by support functions needs to be closely controlled to ensure it adds value. For example, upgrading from a bookkeeper to a financial manager must come with added value, such as cash flow and funding management.

Support functions require clear objectives to be set for them if they are to add value. Their performance must be closely monitored. Involve the line functions in the setting of these objectives and ask how satisfied they are with the services offered. As a rule of thumb, keep the support functions lean to ensure a focus on core functions.

Unfortunately, support functions can evolve into non-value-adding entities that suck up resources and create resentment throughout the organization. When this happens, it is time for a change. The first place to look for change is with the specific support function manager. Can the current manager deliver the change required to turn the service function around, or is the problem *because* of them? Changing the manager will signal to the rest of the organization that you are serious about changing the function. When turning a support function around, start by defining the services required from a zero base. Get the line functions involved in defining the services they want from the support function. Only deliver those services that make it onto the list.

PROCUREMENT

The main functions of procurement are:

- Managing the ordering and receiving of goods and services, including handling procurement data. Their focus is to maximize the efficiency of the transaction.

- Supporting the vendor engagement and contracting process, which is largely tactical and transactionally focused.

- Ensuring that procurement supports the overall organizational strategy.

Below are some questions to help in your review:

- What procurement functionality do you need for your organization to deliver your strategy effectively?

- Is your procurement function efficient? Does your procurement function ensure that you have the best strategic supply partners?

- What functionality do you currently have, and how effective are these functions?

- What additional processes, policies, governance, or systems do you need for your procurement function?

- Can you outsource any of your procurement functions?

- What additional procurement resources do you require?

INFORMATION TECHNOLOGY (IT)

The IT function enables employees to communicate and collaborate. It provides systems that help ensure efficient performance of duties by providing functionality and automating routine tasks.

There are three basic abilities that IT brings to an organization, namely, providing access to information (through data), providing a logical workflow model, and providing networking capabilities:

- **Information** (data) is captured in templates as it is generated, providing instant access to information.

- **A logical workflow model** maps out various tasks and policies into rules, responsibilities, roles, and permissions. Tasks are then performed in the correct sequence by the right person using the right resource.

- **Networks** allow for integration across the organization, including at different locations. It can be extended to suppliers, partners, agents, distributors, and customers.

The IT function has three primary roles:

- **Governance:** Enabling the use of IT systems, architecture, and networks through the implementation of rules and procedures. This includes IT security and data assurance.

- **Infrastructure:** Ensuring that the hardware, networks, and equipment meet the needs of the organization and are in good operational order.

- **Functionality:** Ensuring that the functional needs of the organization are met through software or applications, data management, and security.

Information is key to managing an organization successfully. Such information can be obtained informally (for example, through networks or clients) or formally through management information systems (MIS). The key objective of MIS is to provide useful information quickly and accurately to support decision-making. Excellent information can be considered a key input to competitive advantage.

The first information system installed in an organization is typically one that covers financial transactions. However, this should only be the beginning of the organization's information systems, with the end objective being to capture *all* information critical to the organization's management.

Like anything else, an organization has to learn and mature in its understanding and use of any MIS solution. Installing a comprehensive system when the organization is not ready is a recipe for disaster. All organizations need to go through several stages before reaching MIS maturity. The lowest level of maturity – the **initial** stage – is where the organization lacks clearly defined and documented processes. Success depends on individual effort. The next level up, the **repeatable** stage, is where the organization has basic, repeatable processes with the appropriate discipline in place to ensure their implementation. The **defined** stage is where software is in place to manage all aspects of the organization. Activities are documented, standardized, and integrated into a standard software process. The next stage is the **managed** stage. Here we are looking at the level of information provided by MIS and the use thereof. MIS output is comprehensive, understood, and used to manage the organization. The final stage is one of **continuous improvement**. An organization cannot jump from the initial stage to the continuous improvement stage without going through the intervening stages. You need to bear this in mind when you are reviewing your MIS plans and designs.

Below are some questions to help in your review:

- What are the organization's information needs? How can technology enable your processes? How well are needs currently met? The following actions will help improve your management information systems.

  - List all key management decisions made on an ongoing basis by all employees, for example, expenditure priorities, pricing decisions, performance interventions, and employee effort.

  - List the supporting information required to make better decisions.

  - Review the information. Ask why the information is needed. Does it support organizational goals? Is it too much or too little information?

  - Where does the information originate? Rate the information readily available to help make the decision as Excellent, Good, Mediocre, or Non-existent.

  - List the organization's current business processes and information systems. Look at where you can eliminate bureaucratic practices, for example, those that could reduce paperwork and unnecessary procedures or eliminate policies and practices that demean or belittle human dignity. What can be automated? How good are these systems? Rate them as Excellent, Good, or Poor.

- What needs to be done to improve the availability of information? Ask your employees where to make improvements.
  o Identify improvements to current processes and systems.
  o Determine where additional systems or processes are required to support management information.
- How will new systems be developed, implemented, and supported? How will staff be trained?
- What additional technology do you need to deliver your MIS requirements?
- Determine at what level of maturity your organization is in terms of the five stages outlined above. How will this impact your implementation plans?
- Do you need an expert to review your information systems and discuss plans to ensure that your information systems support your strategy?
- What role and function should the IT function provide? This could include hardware management, systems or software development and management, security and risk-management, information and technology architecture, and user support.
- Can you improve any of your existing IT functions?
- Can you outsource any of your IT functions?
- What additional resources can be allocated to IT the function?

HUMAN RESOURCES

The primary purpose of human resources is to have a workforce ready to meet current operational needs, as well as planning and preparing for the future workforce required to deliver the organization's vision. The main functions of human resource management include:

- Competitive remuneration and reward.
- The planning, recruitment, and selection of a competent workforce.
- Creating a learning environment specific to the organization.
- Ensuring an understanding of the culture and people practices.
- Performance management through regular reviews and ongoing development.
- Leadership and management development and continuity planning.
- Ensuring the health and well-being of employees.

Below are some questions to help in your review:

- Can you achieve your strategy with your current staff, or do you need new staff and skills?
- How are you going to recruit, onboard, retain and train staff to meet your requirements?
- What processes do you have in place to support your workforce?
- What processes do you have in place to meet regulatory people requirements?

- What needs must the HR function meet, both now and in the future?

- How well is the HR function currently meeting these needs?

- What changes must be made to the HR function going forward?

- What additional processes, policies, governance, or systems does the HR function require?

- Can you improve or introduce self-help HR practices?

- Can you outsource any of the HR functions?

- What additional HR resources do you require?

FINANCE

The finance function has two key focus areas: financial manager and accountant.

The **financial manager** helps the organization achieve its financial goals by determining strategies to improve the organization's financial health and to maximize profits. They assist in investment decisions (operations, capital, and securities) and financing options. They produce financial forecasts (projected revenues, expenditures, and cash flows) and they optimize funding (debt and equity).

The financial manager works closely with the accountant. The **accountant** has three areas of focus:

- *Financial accounting*: the preparation of financial statements and reports primarily for external stakeholders, such as shareholders, creditors, regulatory authorities. These financial statements indicate the historical financial position of the organization over a fixed period of time.

- *Management accounting*: the preparation of financial information and reports for internal users to assist in the daily running of the organization. Such reports are forward looking and are focused on the achievement of organizational objectives.

- *Cost accounting*: this is a subset of management accounting that focuses on the cost of, for example, products, operations, or functions.

Below are some questions to help in your review:

- What financial management and accounting functionality do you need for your organization to deliver your strategy?

- What functionality do you currently have, and how effective are these functions?

- What are your current financial controls? How would you improve on them?

- How effectively is your organization financed? How will this change as your organization grows?

- How effective is your organization at planning? How can this be improved?

- What additional processes, policies, governance, or systems do you need for the finance function?

- Can you outsource any of your finance functions?

- What additional finance resources do you require?

7.2 Resources to Deliver

AWARENESS

Resources are an organization's assets, made up of *people*; *plant, warehousing, shop, and office space*; *real estate*; and *financing*.

Insufficient resources or the inappropriate allocation of resources are the biggest reasons that strategies fail to be implemented. Will your current resources be sufficient to deliver your vision? Are your resources optimally allocated to achieve your strategy?

ACTION

In addition to the actions, assets are listed by asset type, and a number of questions are asked of each class for your consideration.

Steps to determine the assets you require are:

- Go through each of the resource topics listed below and determine which resources you need to deliver your strategy. Are there any other resources not listed?

- Review your current resources and their ability to deliver your strategy.

- Determine your resource shortfall for each area.

- Determine strategies to ensure that you have the resources you need to deliver your strategy.

- Determine where you are unlikely to get the resources you require (for instance, you might lack sufficient funds). Determine alternative strategies to source these resources. Investigate how you can use different resources to achieve your strategy. Treat constraints as an opportunity to think out of the box and to be creative. Aim to come up with a completely different solution that can work within the constraints.

- If you still cannot find a way to source the required resources, then consider trade-offs. What needs to be dropped from your strategy because of resource constraints? What aspects of the strategy need to change?

- Update your strategy, where necessary.

- Review how resources are allocated in your budgets. Re-allocate resources where appropriate. (See *BUDGETING*)

People

- Do you and your management team have the necessary abilities to deliver your vision?

- What distinctive staffing capabilities and expertise do you need?

- Can you get more out of your current workforce?

- What staffing number do you need?

- Which of the identified roles/positions can be filled with your current staff?

- How do you intend to fill the shortfall? (for example, through recruitment, training, temporary staff, contractors)

Plant, warehousing, shop, office space

Facilities
- What are the ideal facilities you need to meet your growth forecasts?

- What are your current facilities? What is their operational state? How well do they serve your organization in meeting your growth forecasts? Ask yourself: Are they suited to your type of business? Do they give you a competitive edge? Can they cope with future changes in technology? Consider safety, environment, occupation and health requirements, image, and the affordability, resale, or salvage of equipment at the end of its life.

- Determine a plan to upgrade your facilities to meet your growth forecasts, including the procurement process (how, when, and where).

- How will you finance (purchase, lease, hire) these new facilities?

- Identify your non-performing equipment. What can you do to increase performance? Should you be getting rid of any equipment?

- Can you increase revenue from your equipment? Consider any underutilized physical assets and unexploited intellectual capital.

Layout
- How are your operations laid out? Is this optimal for your business? Ask yourself whether it adds to efficiency and effectiveness, allows for the free flow of materials, encourages customer shopping, and provides a professional look and feel.

Maintenance
- Do you have a maintenance plan to keep your assets operating at the required level?

- What are the cost implications of planned maintenance versus fixing breakdowns?

- How do you plan to keep the equipment and locations projecting the image you want for the organization? For example, clean delivery trucks or the look and feel of customer facilities.

Capacity

- What are the current capacities? What are the lead and lag times?

- How can you increase capacities or efficiencies to meet seasonal demand changes? For example, you might want to look at your internal capacity vs. subcontracting.

- How will operations be maintained during peak demand times?

Work environment

- What can you do to make your work environment a safer place?

- Keep things spotless – improve housekeeping (keep toilets and personal spaces clean, remove staff reserved parking spaces).

Real estate

- Review your current real estate. Is it appropriate for your needs? Will it meet your future needs? What do you need to do in light of your conclusions?

- What are the drivers and priorities of location for your organization? Is it, for example, convenience to customers, convenience to suppliers of raw materials, source of labor, proximity to transport, access to water or power, or costs?

- Are there any legislative requirements that encourage or dissuade the location of your organization? For example, tax breaks or planning requirements.

- Where is the organization currently located? Why was this location selected? Is this still relevant? If not, what are the alternative locations?

- What is the ideal location to suit your organization's requirements? What are the costs to move? How will you finance this move? Should you move? By when? Undertake a detailed analysis to help you decide.

- Can you increase revenue from your real estate?

Financing

- What additional financing will you require to fund your growth in order to achieve your vision?

- How effective is your current financing model? How can you improve it?

BUDGETING

The allocation of resources is a key component in implementing a strategy. Resource allocation is often done through budgets. Review your budgets to ensure that they are aligned with your vision and strategy.

HOW TO BUDGET

1. Start by determining your **sources of income**. What are your different sources of income? Do you expect these to continue? What type of growth do you forecast? What additional sources of income do you plan to attract in the coming year?

2. Determine your fixed expenses. What expenses will happen no matter what happens to your sales? This would include finance charges, leases, rentals, and payroll expenses.

3. Determine your variable expenses. Variable expenses are all those costs that are not fixed. Some of these will be directly linked to your sales, such as the cost of goods sold or produced. Some might be project- or activity-based, for example, a new marketing campaign, training, or travel expenses to a conference. Be aware of the impact that cutting any of these will have on your organization as a whole.

4. Determine any once-off expenses. These generally consist of capital costs, such as buying a new production plant or a balloon payment on a lease.

5. Put your income and expenses together in a typical income statement, balance sheet, and cash flow format. Calculate missing items like interest and taxes.

6. Review the above and ask yourself whether there are any other cash flow considerations that you need to be aware of, such as cash flow deficits, impacts of bulk buying, or a change in credit policy.

7. Ask whether the budget will help to achieve your strategy? What changes need to occur to align your budget better to your vision?

ZERO-BASED BUDGETING

Peter Pyhrr, who developed and implemented zero-based budgeting at Texas Instruments in the 1960s, defined zero-based budgeting as a method of budgeting that involves preparing the budget from scratch with a zero base. It consists of re-evaluating every line item and justifying all the expenditure that it might incur, regardless of how much money has previously been budgeted or spent in the past. Under this method, every activity needs to be justified, explaining the revenue that every cost will generate for the organization.

To apply zero-based budgeting in your organization, start by identifying all the tasks in an area and then the means of completing each task. Next, review *alternatives* to completing the task to find the best approach. Remember, your budget must be aligned with achieving your strategy. Cost the approach. This then becomes the budget.

Zero-based budgeting has the advantages of greater accuracy and efficiency, more focused operations reducing redundant activities and costs, and a higher likelihood of disciplined execution. However, it is time consuming, can be expensive, requires high manager involvement, and does require a certain level of expertise.

It is a tool that can be used every three to five years rather than annually, depending on the individual circumstances of each organization.

7.3 Your Delivery Partners

AWARENESS

Delivery partners include all suppliers that provide you with inputs or services. Partners could include:

- Supply partners of products or raw materials.

- Marketing partners that help in selling or act as referrals for your products or services.

- Delivery partners that help deliver customer solutions.

- Distribution partners that help deliver customer orders.

- Financing partners, including accountants, investors, financial advisors, and bankers.

- Technology partners that help deliver technology solutions either for your organization or for your customers.

- Outsourcing partners.

Strategic delivery partners – especially suppliers – need to be treated as an integral part of the organization. Successful companies often work together with their suppliers to solve the needs of their customers. Good supplier partnerships are developed to benefit both organizations and are based on mutual respect and trust. These partnerships can help to reduce potential problems (like quality, late delivery, and late payment) for the organization and its customers.

ACTION

The following actions will help to improve the management of your delivery partners.

- Perform a review of your strategic delivery partners.
  - Identify each of your delivery partners.
  - List the service they provide.
  - Rate each partner in terms of:
    - o How essential they are in delivering your strategy. Score as follows: *not essential*; *important but not essential*, or *essential (could not do without them)*.
    - o How easy it is to replace them. Score as follows: *easy to replace*; *could replace but with difficulty*, or *almost impossible to replace*.
  - Analyze your review and determine which of your delivery partners are strategic.
  - Focusing on your *strategic* delivery partners first. List what you would ideally want from them. Repeat the process for all your organization's non-strategic delivery partners once you are managing your strategic delivery partners effectively.
  - Score your strategic partners' performance in terms of what you require of them. Score as follows: *poor service*; *okay service with room for improvement*, or *excellent service*. You can also score your other partners but focus initially on your strategic ones.
  - Determine your strategies and actions to optimize the management of your strategic partners.
- Define plans and actions to manage your strategic delivery partners. Can any of your delivery partner relationships

be formed into sources of competitive advantage for your organization? Can you have exclusivity agreements with any of these partners? What can you do to work better with these partners? (See *DOs AND DON'Ts OF ALLIANCES*)

- Talk to your strategic suppliers to find out what they think of you as a customer. What do they want in a customer? How do you measure up? How can you work better together? How can they help your organization – for example, with ideas, information, products, problem-solving, improved terms, or minimum stock holdings? (See *PURCHASING STRATEGIES*).

- Invite your suppliers to your organization to see how you use their products. Ask them how they can help improve your organization.

- Talk to your other strategic delivery partners to determine how you can work together in the future.

- Replace underperforming, non-critical suppliers.

- Review your value chain and structure to identify areas that can be outsourced. Find potential suppliers of these services.

- Review suppliers to whom you currently outsource work and determine whether it would make more sense to insource such services.

- Regularly communicate your plans and progress with your suppliers. Remember to ask for their help in developing your organization further.

- Find out-of-the-box solutions with your suppliers that will solve both your and their challenges.

- Ensure that you are identifying and managing your strategic delivery partners on an ongoing basis.

- Improve your mechanisms to ensure continuous feedback from your delivery partners.

DOs AND DON'Ts OF ALLIANCES

Dos:
- Form an alliance where you can exploit one of your unique strengths.

- Form an alliance where you can take advantage of the partner's unique strengths.

- Form an alliance when neither partner has the desire or ability to acquire the other's unique strength.

- Always form an alliance around capabilities.

Don'ts:
- Don't form an alliance to correct a weakness.

- Don't form an alliance where the partner is trying to negate their weakness.

- Never form an alliance where you give away your priority technology, skills, or expertise.

- Don't form an alliance around products or markets. Alliances formed to exploit the similarity of certain products or markets rarely work.

PURCHASING STRATEGIES

The *Portfolio Purchasing Model*[22] created by Peter Kraljic looks at selecting the most appropriate purchasing strategies for different types of products. It uses two dimensions to analyze your product: *Impact on financial results* and *Supply risk* (or uncertainty).

The resulting model is shown in the figure below:

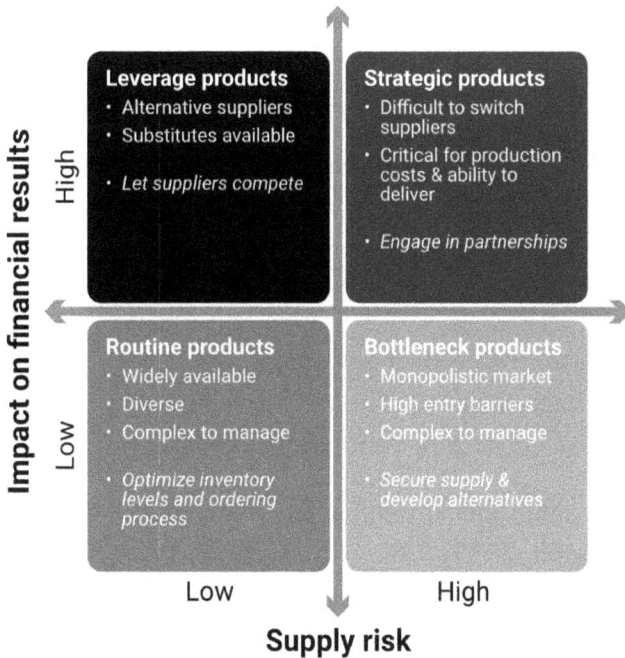

Kraljic's Purchasing Model

---

22   Steve ten Have, Wouter ten Have, Frans Stevens and Marcel van der Elst, Key Management Models, FT Press, 2003.

The steps to follow to undertake this analysis are:

1. Group your products logically. This is not as easy as it sounds. A good starting point might be to start with product by supplier. To assist with grouping, ask yourself whether any product could be purchased just as easily from another supplier.

2. For each product group, determine the impact it has on your organization's financial results. This might be determined by factors like the product's direct costs, the percentage of total costs in the end product, and the indirect cost of purchasing. Score each with a *high* or *low*.

3. Determine the supply risk for each product group. Risk determinates include the number of suppliers, the availability of reserves and alternatives, the stability of the supplier, and the cost of switching to an alternative supplier. Score each with a simple *high* or *low*.

4. Allocate the product grouping to the matrix, as detailed in the diagram above. You now have an overarching strategy to manage each of your product groupings.

Where your product grouping falls in the matrix will determine your strategy:

- **High Financial Impact and High Supply Risk**

These are your strategic items requiring the most focus. You want to develop long-term supply relationships and plan for contingencies. Items falling in this quadrant require regular review.

- **High Supply Risk and Low Financial Impact**

Typically, this is where supply is unreliable. Consider placing larger orders to ensure that you have available stock, or developing product alternatives.

- **High Financial Impact and Low Risk**

Allow suppliers to compete. You can easily substitute your suppliers, so push for the best terms possible. Look for more cost-effective products.

- **Low Risk and Low Financial Impact**

These are non-critical items. Optimize your order volumes and inventory levels. Ask whether you can automate the purchasing process.

7.4 Your Structure

AWARENESS

Structure is a system that outlines how your value chain activities are to be directed in order to achieve the vision and strategy. A poor structure can destroy an organization. The primary rationale of any organization is to satisfy customers. Therefore, it makes sense that the structure supports such objectives by being close to the customer. How you service your customers is defined in your value chain. Your value chain thus becomes a key input when defining your structure.

Populating your structure becomes your next priority. As the CEO or owner, if you are critical to your organization's future growth, make sure you stay close to the customer as the organization grows. Avoid getting caught up in becoming an administrator. Employ someone else to do that for you. Don't create positions just to accommodate the people currently working for you. If they don't fit into your new structure, you will have to make some hard decisions as to their future role in the organization.

ACTION

The following actions will improve your structure:

- Review your strategy and target value chain and think about how you would design a structure to support them. (See *STRUCTURE TIPS, DESIGN THINKING STRUCTURE*, and *STRUCTURE OPTIONS*)
- Start with a clean sheet of paper and draft a structure that will support your growth aspirations and plans.
- Compare the revised structure with your current structure. Is it telling you anything?
- Compare your proposed structure with other organizations that you feel operate well. What does it tell you?
- Discuss the structure with key employees and ask for their input.
- Once you have decided to change your structure, do it immediately. Don't drag the process of change out thus causing uncertainty.
- Finalize the structure, populate it, and communicate it. Make sure everyone knows where they fit in by defining rules, roles, and responsibilities.

STRUCTURE TIPS

There is no one set of rules to define an ideal structure. This is because there is no ideal structure. Go with what works for you. Your structure is not the be-all of your organization. It cannot deliver operational excellence – that is up to you and your team. At the same time, don't change your structure unless there is a compelling reason to do so.

There are, however, several design principles that you can take into consideration when designing or reviewing your structure:

- Build the structure around the work to be done or your processes, not around your people.

- Minimize the handover of uncompleted work between different parts of your structure.

- Optimize the number of people managed by one person. You don't want a manager only managing one person, nor do you want them managing too many people.

- Make sure that responsibility for an area of work resides with one person only. There must be no room for *not* taking responsibility.

- Get the right balance between core and support activities. Support must enable core, but not to the extent that it gets in the way of effective delivery.

DESIGN THINKING STRUCTURE

Since design thinking is all about balancing intuitive thinking and analytical thinking (while also being both explorative and exploitative), how do you bring this balance into an organization's structure?

There will always be a place for set work and the accomplishment of such work. Identify such areas in your organization and structure these areas accordingly with defined structure, positions, and job descriptions. They could form the predominant structure, depending on your core business.

There will also be a place for work that is structured around projects. In fact, your organization might deliver its core work through projects. In this instance, you might have a more complex project-based structure, such as a matrix structure. (See *STRUCTURE OPTIONS*)

No matter what your core focus is, internal projects will exist to improve delivery. They could, for example, be projects to develop new products or projects to improve performance. Such projects are continually being established and closed. The people involved would, in all likelihood, need to be delivering these projects over and above their normal work. To accommodate such projects, your structure would therefore need to be flexible.

Your managers' prime job is to put out fires while managing their department's routine delivery. Processes are defined at a fixed point of time depending on circumstances, and your managers need to identify changing customer requirements and to adapt their processes accordingly. Managers are there to solve problems and improve how you conduct your business as efficiently as possible. They will often have to establish projects to solve problems as they arise. If they are there purely to manage fixed processes, they will, in all likelihood, miss changes in the market. Should your organization fail to adapt to meet these changing needs, it will quickly lose relevance.

Moving toward a structure that supports design thinking often requires changes to processes and company culture.

Over time, many organizations tend to favor analytical thinking over intuitive thinking. This is often because analytical and exploitative approaches are easier to monitor, administer, and manage. The intuitive and explorative elements fall away, to the long-term detriment of the organization. This is something you need to be aware of continually.

STRUCTURE OPTIONS

The most familiar structure is one of hierarchy. It can be highly hierarchical with many layers of management or flatter with more autonomy allowed. I am willing to bet that organizations that are highly frustrating to work with (like traditional banks or governmental organizations) are also highly hierarchical.

The focus of the hierarchy (or structure) can change between organizations and is often based on a number of factors. The most common include:

- **Functional** structure: This is organized around people with similar skills, for example, marketing, sales, manufacturing, and finance. The drawback of such a structure is often coordination and communications between functions, where structural boundaries create fictional barriers to getting the job done.

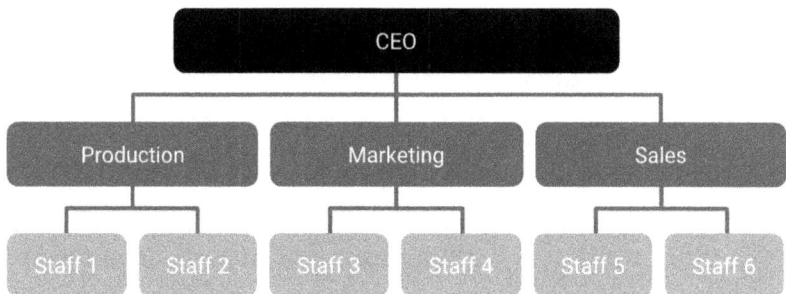

A Structure Based on Function

- **Divisional** structure: Typically, this is where organizations are structured around different business areas. For example, a food company might structure itself around events (like weddings, corporate events, walk-in trade). Coordination and communication are drawbacks of such a structure. You might also find a duplication of functions (for example, each department might feel the need to employ their own bookkeeper) as well as excess capacity (for example, one division might grow their capabilities rather than look for spare capacity in other divisions).

- Some organizations design their structure around **product**, **process**, and **region**. These are typically variations on functional and divisional structures, with each having its pros and cons.

- A more complex structure is the **matrix** structure. It combines elements of the functional structure with the divisional structure. I once worked for a company with a matrix structure. Before changing to the matrix structure, advisory work was delivered through areas of specialization. Projects were often delivered using skills across the areas of specialization, which caused project stresses between the specialization areas. Customers were also demanding industry specialization, not just skills specialization. A matrix structure was introduced where each person had an industry and skills specialization. Team leaders were appointed for the different industry areas with a focus on developing market opportunities (in other words, sales). Other team leaders were appointed to ensure the recruitment and development of skilled staff. There was a third element of management for the delivery of projects within an industry specialization but across skills. Support functions continued to be managed based on their functions. While such a matrix structure has many advantages, it is complex to manage.

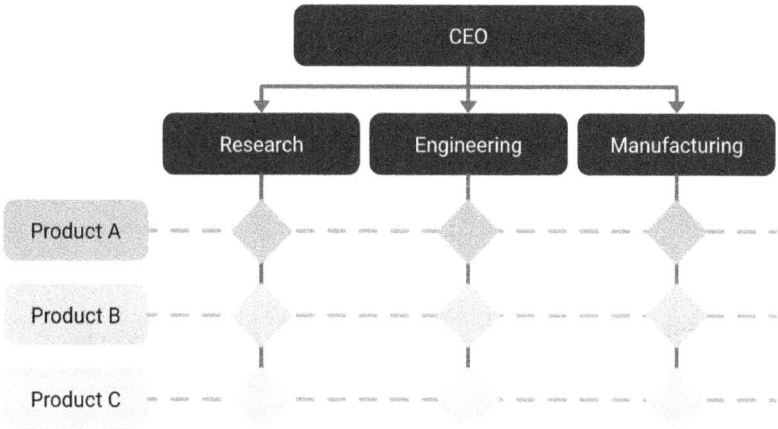

A Matrix Structure

There is no one correct answer for how an organization should be structured. You have to design a structure that not only works for you but also enables and enhances your customer experience by meeting their continually changing needs.

The structures of the future will be those that are agile and continuously changing to meet changing customer needs and external dynamics. They will enable greater teamwork, communication, and information flow while empowering the workforce. Leadership will need to evolve to support these structures and to reward innovation, learning, experimenting, and design thinking.

8

Efficiency and Effectiveness

This module's focus is on efficiency and effectiveness. Your workforce is always going to have the biggest impact on efficiency and effectiveness. The first area of focus is getting the most out of your employees.

This module then reviews various approaches to improving efficiencies. The final area of focus is on measuring performance and includes tactics for different sales performance scenarios and turnaround situations.

8.1 Your Employees as Partners

AWARENESS

Great organizations are all about great people. As the CEO or owner of your organization, your aim is to recruit and retain an outstanding workforce. Your employees are looking for quality jobs that provide adequate compensation. A quality job includes opportunities to learn, a variety of tasks, an ability to maintain integrity and self-esteem, and a balance between work and life.

There are many theories about effective employee management. The difficulty comes in applying them, especially in a fast-growing business. How you treat your employees will have a direct impact on how they treat your customers.

Getting employees engaged requires a balance of three things: employees need to feel that they have autonomy or freedom to be creative, that they are good at what they do, and that their work serves a purpose.

The key elements of building your employees as partners are:

- Recruit the right people.
- Set out precisely what is expected of them.
- Provide ongoing formal and informal training.
- Give your employees complete authority to run their area of business – let them make the required decisions while you observe and coach.
- Continually communicate and provide feedback on their performance.

- Reward good performance and take remedial action against poor performance.

- Provide quality jobs (quality jobs are those that provide opportunities to learn, have variety, do not compromise integrity and self-esteem, and encourage a healthy work-life balance.)

With your employees, you want to:

- Create a sense of purpose. Have a compelling vision for the organization to which employees feel connected.

- Create a sense of competence. Ongoing learning is essential to ensuring competence.

- Create a feeling of control. Employees need to feel that they are in control of their lives and are not mere pawns in the larger scheme of things.

- Create a sense that they are making a difference. Each staff member must feel convinced that the work they do genuinely makes a difference to the organization's overall performance.

- Create a sense of belonging, a feeling of community – that they are part of the business. This includes trust, mutual respect, and a preparedness to help others.

- Create a sense of enjoyment. Having fun and being playful is essential to both the mental and organizational wellbeing of your employees.

- Create a sense of meaning, where work can be seen as improving the quality of life, helping others, or contributing something to society.

The business owner can be a key factor in an organization's performance. In the organization's early days, the entrepreneur needs to do everything. As an organization grows and new employees are brought on board, the entrepreneur needs to delegate and empower their team. Letting go is a psychological issue, not a business one.

When the owner's inability to let go interferes with the daily running of the organization, it becomes a business issue. Employees become demotivated by the owner's continual interference, overriding decisions, changing direction – and needing to be aware of their boss's mood. When this happens, they stop doing their jobs, leaving the owner with more and more pressures and responsibilities. The result is high employee turnover, an exhausted owner, and deteriorating customer service.

Adapted from David Hall and Dinah Bennett's *The Hallmarks for Successful Business*.

ACTION

The following actions will help to improve your employees' involvement and performance.

- Spend time recruiting the best. (See *EMPLOYMENT TIPS*)

- Set clear expectations of what you expect of employees. (See *PEOPLE MANAGEMENT*)

- You want your employees to add value to the organization – train and coach them to do so.

- Analyze your employees' performance in terms of productivity and use of their potential. Build your organization around the best performers while taking remedial action against poor performers.

- Find additional ways to incentivize your employees. Small gestures can mean far more than their cost to the organization.

- Improve the quality of the individual employee's work environment. Make sure they understand the purpose of their job and how it contributes to the organization's success. Ensure that the environment provides the employee with a sense of meaning and adding value. Be sure that they have the necessary competence to do the job and that they are in control of how they execute their responsibilities. Finally, make sure that they feel that they belong and that they enjoy working for your organization.

- Undertake a climate survey.

- Review the makeup of your management team and the roles each person plays. Determine gaps in skills and determine what actions to take. (See *MANAGEMENT ROLES*)

- Use diversity and inclusion as a means of improving business performance. (See *DIVERSITY AND INCLUSION*)

EMPLOYMENT TIPS

RECRUITING

Spend time recruiting the best people by following a systematic hiring process:

- Identify the purpose of hiring a new person.

- Put together a job definition.

- Define the tasks required for the position.

- Prioritize these tasks.

- Define the competencies and qualifications required for the position.

- Look for potential recruits. Consider offering bonuses to current employees who bring successful candidates on board.

- Conduct interviews. The following are some tips for the recruitment process:

  - Recruiting is a line responsibility. Short-listed candidates should be interviewed by seniors, peers, and even subordinates. Start the process of handing over recruitment slowly by including the line in interviews and gradually handing over.

  - Don't disrespect the candidate by canceling interviews or keeping them waiting. Finding the correct employee is one of the most crucial activities for your organization. Do it right!

  - Prepare for the interview by developing questions to ask candidates. Identify selection criteria appropriate to your organization (for example, skills, attitude, teamwork potential, customer orientation). Look at your star employees – what makes them successful in your organization? What traits or values do they display that make them successful? These could be hard traits such as skills or softer qualities such as teamwork. What behavior do you require of a recruit? Design interview questions around these traits and behaviors.

  - Develop a scoring process based on the set questions you want to ask.

- During the interview, ask the candidate for examples of where they have shown the specific traits and behaviors you are looking for.

- Make sure any recruit is passionate about *why* you are in business. You want to hire employees who are already motivated and inspire them with your *Why*.

- Score each candidate as per your scoring process.

- Hire the candidate of choice and formally onboard them into the organization.

- Evaluate the new employee's performance. You might want to do this more regularly than you would with longer-serving employees.

SETTING EXPECTATIONS

- Three staples used to manage and control people are:

  - The setting of objectives.

  - Performance appraisals.

  - Job descriptions.

- These staples can do more harm than good when done incorrectly. Review your practices to simplify the processes. Focus on what is essential – you might need to be flexible rather than defining rigid processes. Make sure that your processes are helping you to get the most out of employees but not at the expense of treating employees civilly.

- Make objective-setting a bottom-up process. Ask your employees how they are going to help deliver on the objectives and strategies you have set for your organization. Review each suggestion to ensure it aligns with what you are trying to achieve. To get the most out of an employee, try to align the objectives you want to set for them with their personal goals and objectives.

- Analyze each employee's performance in terms of productivity and the use of their potential. Build your organization around the best performers while taking remedial action against the poor performers.

- Ask your employees to review the performance of the management team. Get feedback on:

  - What management does well

  - What they do poorly

  - Where they can improve

  - What training they should attend

- Typically, a job description includes a job title and a summary of the nature of the job, the purpose and objectives of the job, major duties, the scope and limit of authority, specific mental or physical requirements for the position, and necessary qualifications.

- The three staple processes should be used continually and not just annually. Review performance regularly, set new objectives as circumstances change, and make sure that job descriptions are flexible to cater to changing circumstances.

TRAINING

- If you want your employees to add value to the organization, you need to train and coach them to do so.

- Continuously look to retrain employees *before* it becomes necessary. Don't just train blindly – make sure the training is relevant to the skills required to overcome the challenges of the job.

- Review your current pool of skills: Do you want more people to have these skills? What skills are missing? The results of this review should drive your training agenda.

- Training must be line-driven. Get line to design and deliver training or identify additional skills they require where they cannot train themselves.

- Are there government employment or training incentives you can take advantage of?

REWARDS

- Rewards can depend on where you are in your businesses life cycle:

  - In the *start-up phase*, there is less emphasis on salary and perks and more emphasis on long-term incentives such as share options.

  - In the *growth phase*, there is still an emphasis on long-term incentives but with an increasing emphasis on promoting short-term results. It is a chance to catch up on benefits and salaries.

  - In the *mature phase*, most of the emphasis is on keeping salaries and perks competitive. There is less concern for long-term benefits. Bonuses are used to boost productivity.

  - During *aging*, benefits and salaries are most important. Very little goes to long-term benefits and growth incentives.

- Find out additional ways to incentivize your employees. Small gestures can mean far more than their cost.

- Average pay yields average work. Look at how you can pay above the average through performance incentives that will reinforce the behavior you want. Incentives only work if the person believes they can influence the results.

- Study successful incentive schemes inside and outside of your industry for ideas.

- Tie incentives to the performance of work teams.

- Makes sure your incentives encourage design thinking.

- When introducing incentives, provide ongoing performance feedback at least once a month.

- A new incentive scheme can be too complicated to implement to obtain the desired results. Do it slowly, phasing it in over a three- to five-year period.

QUALITY JOBS

- Do something memorable for your people that they will remember long after the event.

- Involve everyone in almost everything. There are no limits on the ability of properly selected, well-trained, adequately supported, well-paid, committed people. For example, involve your employees in quality improvement and self-inspection, cost reduction, measuring and monitoring results, budget development, work area layout, new technology assessment, recruitment, and customer calls and visits.

- Evaluate whether any supervisory roles can be performed by lower-level employees. Empower your employees to take responsibility for their work and outputs.

- Ask employees to talk about possible improvements to the way they work.

- Initially, mistakes will be made as you empower your workforce. While encouraging your people to take risks (to promote risk-taking for continuous improvement), offer employment security. Look at providing employment guarantees to a large portion of the workforce after a suitable probationary period.

Adapted in part from Tom Peters' Thriving on Chaos, as well as from Peter Wilson and Sue Bates' *The Essential Guide to Managing Small Business Growth.*

PEOPLE MANAGEMENT

Always deal with your employees with *empathy*. A person in a new position will always know less than the previous incumbent. Encourage your employees by asking how you can help them. When an employee's performance declines, start by asking whether everything is alright. By showing empathy you will contribute toward greater job satisfaction, a caring organization and ultimately, a more successful one. Get your managers also to deal with employees with empathy.

The following tips can be used to improve your employee interactions:

RULES FOR SUCCESSFUL EMPLOYEE INTERACTIONS

- Always aim at maintaining or enhancing the self-esteem of the person you are interacting with.

- Never attack the person. Play the ball and not the person by focusing on the problem.

- Never make any assumptions, even if you think they might have committed an offense.

- Encourage the person to express their opinions and make suggestions.

- Allow the person sufficient time to think through the problem and suggest a solution. Don't expect them to have answers right now!

- Ensure that there is an actionable program for the person to follow.

- Always set a follow-up date and diarize it.

STEPS TO RECOGNIZE SATISFACTORY BEHAVIOR

The purpose of these steps is to encourage the continuation of good performance and motivate the employee.

1. Tell the employee specifically what they have done that deserves recognition and why.

2. Say that you appreciate what they have done.

3. Explain why it is important that they continue to maintain their level of work performance.

4. Ask if there is anything you can do to help them maintain their performance standards.

5. If applicable, define steps each of you can take. Set a follow-up date and diarize it.

STEPS TO IMPROVE INADEQUATE PERFORMANCE

Follow these steps to address an employee's inadequate work performance or unacceptable personal work habits:

1. Explain to the employee what you have observed, why it is unacceptable, or why it concerns you.

2. Ask for and listen openly to the employee's explanation. Decide on its validity.

3. State your performance or behavior requirements of them.

4. Guide them to formulate a program to improve their performance or behavior to your required standard. If it is a repeat situation where the employee is still not performing according to expectation, you might skip to the specific disciplinary action you will now be required to take.

5. Offer your help in meeting your performance or behavior requirements.

6. If applicable, indicate what disciplinary action will be taken if they do not meet your performance or behavior requirements.

7. Assure the employee of your support and agree on what steps each of you will take, including a diarized follow-up date.

STEPS FOR CONDUCTING A PERFORMANCE APPRAISAL

The following steps can be used when conducting a performance appraisal:

1. Recap the objectives that were set for the employee.

2. Ask the employee how well they feel they have done in achieving their objectives.

3. Recognize any achievements made.

4. Ask and listen closely to their explanation of why uncompleted objectives were not achieved.

5. Ask for suggestions for achieving uncompleted objectives.

6. Tell the employee where you think they can improve on their performance. Express your confidence in their ability to achieve their objectives. Build on their strengths.

7. Ask the employee about their career and developmental objectives and discuss how these can be met in their current position.

8. Where necessary, set new objectives and determine developmental strategies.

9. Ensure that you have the employee's agreement when setting new objectives and strategies.

10. Together, set action steps that each of you will take, and set (and diarize) a follow-up date.

STEPS FOR CONDUCTING A SALARY REVIEW

A salary review should only be conducted after the completion of a performance review. The steps of the salary review are:

1. Explain the purpose of the session and recap the performance appraisal process and results. Focus on common ground and confirm their agreement of the results.

2. Explain the basis for their overall salary review.

3. Explain that their salary review relates to their performance. Compliment the employee appropriately.

4. Ask the employee for their response and discuss.

5. Summarize your discussions and, if applicable, define steps each of you will take, and set (and diarize) a follow-up date.

STEPS TO HELP MANAGE NEGATIVE CRITICISM

You will, at some stage, be criticized by an employee. You can manage the situation as follows:

1. Listen openly and don't interrupt. Don't defend yourself.

2. Ask for specific examples of what you are being criticized for.

3. Thank the person for raising the issue and summarize your understanding of the issue.

4. Explain your actions, behavior, or decisions without defending yourself and without hostility. Specify those for which you do and do not take accountability.

5. Ask the person for their response and suggestions for resolving the remaining differences of opinion.

6. If appropriate, define steps each of you will take, and set (and diarize) a follow-up date.

MANAGEMENT ROLES

For effective management, an organization needs to bring together a team of leaders with different but complementary skill sets. Management expert Dr. Ichak Adizes developed the *PAEI Model*[23] and defined four different leadership characteristics necessary for an effective management team: *Producer, Administrator, Entrepreneur,* and *Integrator.* Any one person could have skills that cross the four categories defined. Thus, an effective team could have more or less than four members.

---

23   Steve ten Have, Wouter ten Have, Frans Stevens and Marcel van der Elst, Key Management Models, FT Press, 2003.

Adizes' four management roles and typical descriptions of the role are:

- **The Producer** (P): Long hours, restless, serious, little emotion, says things like "do-it-now", "get it done", and "hard work solves all problems", always fighting deadlines, explains by doing, feels that teamwork is less efficient owing to communication needs.

- **The Administrator** (A): Neat, organized, low key, control freak, careful, step-by-step, adhering to rules and procedures, punctual, schedules meetings as a rule rather than for reasons, likes standardization, thinks teams work if they follow team roles.

- **The Entrepreneur** (E): Irregular hours, may (at times) not show up at all, playful, jokes, tells stories, talks, inspires, dreams, exaggerates, does not wait, action-oriented, hopping around, unexpected views, teams are an audience for the entrepreneur's vision.

- **The Integrator** (I): Reliable, trustworthy, warm, caring, good listener, always there, seeks compromise, tries to understand people, empathic, solves problems by talking them through, sees teamwork as a goal in itself.

The importance of each role depends on the situation and the maturity of an organization.

Ask yourself:

- Who in your management team plays each of the roles? Any one person could play multiple roles.

- Are there any role gaps?

- What are the implications of the gaps?

- How important is it that the gaps are filled?

DIVERSITY AND INCLUSION

Diversity consists of the traits and characteristics that make people unique. This includes race, gender, language, religion, age, disability, family status, education, background and experience, ethnicity, and sexual orientation. **Inclusion** is about the behaviors and social norms that ensure people feel welcome.

Unfortunately, not everyone embraces diversity and inclusion, with resistance coming in many forms, both overtly and covertly. Diversity and inclusion, when managed correctly, have impacted an organization's performance positively. A 2015 PwC study[24] found that:

- 85% of CEOs whose organizations have an inclusion and diversity strategy said it had improved their bottom line.

- Fortune 500 companies with a higher representation of women on their boards of directors outperformed their peers by 53% in returns on equity and 42% in returns on sales.

- Organizations with high ratings for inclusion and diversity were 70% more likely to be successful in new markets and 45% more likely to improve their market share.

Review your organization's performance to determine how open you are to diversity and inclusion. You might need an independent reviewer to give you a true picture of the situation. Some questions to ask yourself about your organization's approach to diversity and inclusion include:

---

24   PwC, 2015, The PwC Diversity Journey: Creating Impact, Achieving Results – Executive Summary, PWC, <https://www.pwc.com/gx/en/diversity-inclusion/best-practices/assets/exec-summary-the-pwc-diversity-journey.pdf>.

- Does your organization actively support inclusion and diversity efforts?

- Are diversity and inclusion part of your organization's strategy and values?

- Are your recruitment and advancement processes biased in any way?

- How diverse are your teams?

- Does your organization attract and retain a diverse talent pool?

- Is it safe for minority groups to speak up?

- Do you reward and promote people equally based on the work they do (and not on other criteria)?

Diversity and inclusion are closely interconnected. A focus on one will directly impact the other. It is not a once-off but rather an ongoing process. Some key diversity and inclusion strategies include:

- Ensuring that your leadership team is committed to diversity. You, as CEO or owner, will need to champion any efforts.

- Assigning your leadership team the responsibility for leading and sponsoring your diversity and inclusion program. Hold them responsible for the results too.

- Review your leadership and management team. Does it reflect diversity? While diversity is a numbers game, the mix of your management team reflects how serious you are about tackling diversity issues.

- Review your strategy, values, culture, and brand. Do they all tell the same story while supporting diversity and inclusion?

- Train your people (at all levels) on topics like *unconscious bias*. Every employee must see their role in the organization's culture.

- Review your recruitment, development, performance management, promotion, and reward systems for bias in any way. Remember to look at the employee experience as a whole and at the impacts your various policies and practices might have on each employee. Forget "fit" and focus on how people can thrive in your organization.

- Strengthen your anti-discriminatory policies.

- Make sure you are conscious of diversity and inclusion when planning corporate events. Acknowledge and honor different cultural and religious practices.

- Ask your employees for their inputs on diversity and inclusion. Create conditions where everyone can contribute without fear. Introduce independently facilitated focus groups to understand the challenges faced by your different employee groupings better.

- Enter external awards programs that list diversity and inclusion in their performance criteria.

Organizations are often caught unaware of trouble brewing in this area. While it is better to be prepared in advance, this is not always possible and, when ignored, can quickly turn into a PR disaster.

8.2 Your Internal Efficiencies

AWARENESS

In any organization, there is ongoing pressure to improve efficiencies and reduce costs. Such measures are not about becoming over pedantic about controlling costs, nor are they about retrenching people. It is about doing business better while saving costs.

Business improvement is a continuous process, one the Japanese call *kaizen*, meaning *continuous improvement*. Continued learning and improvement will ultimately result in a more competitive and successful organization.

ACTION

The following actions will help to improve your internal efficiencies:

- Review your business processes. Can you consolidate/ simplify/improve your processes? Ask your employees for their input. (See *BUSINESS PROCESS REVIEW*)

- Review your support functions to get more from them. Do they have the support of line functions? Do you have sufficient support functionality? Do you have too much support?

- Review your overheads and non-core activities and take action based on your results. For each overhead service, ask yourself:

  - Is the cost necessary? Is it critical, desired, or nice to have?

- Does it add value?

- Is the output quality sufficient?

- Is the output quantity sufficient?

- Can it be outsourced at a reasonable cost?

■ Review your working capital policies and practices. (See *WORKING CAPITAL*)

■ Undertake a Pareto analysis of your customers. Can you improve profitability by reducing your customer base? What conclusions can you draw from your customer base? (See *PARETO ANALYSIS*)

■ Undertake a Pareto analysis of your inventory. Can you reduce your inventory levels while increasing customer service? What conclusions can you draw about the items you hold in inventory? (See *PARETO ANALYSIS*)

■ Ask an expert in the field for an independent review of your organization.

■ Research and learn from other organizations in your industry or related industries.

■ Encourage continuous improvement. (See *CONTINUOUS IMPROVEMENT*)

■ Improve your environmental impact. (See *SURVIVING THE CLIMATE CRISIS*)

■ Improve your asset management.

■ Identify a few key projects that can have a quick, significant impact at minimum cost.

■ Monitor progress and continuously encourage ongoing improvement.

■ Inform relevant stakeholders (especially employees) about successes and lessons learned.

BUSINESS PROCESS REVIEW

A business process review is carried out by taking an element of your organization (for example, how a customer purchases from you), reviewing how the process is performed, and then using this information to determine how you can improve your service delivery.

To do this:

1. Ensure that you have a clearly defined strategy and target value chain before you go about redefining any processes.

2. Identify your various business processes and decide on a priority area to address. An existing process is always your starting point.

3. Involve all or a cross-section of employees working in the chosen area.

4. Define the process involved in sequential order. For example, the customer purchase process might take place in the following sequence: (See *PROCESS DEFINITION*)

Customer query	Quote	Order placed	Prepare order	Deliver order	After sales	Payment received

A Typical Customer Purchase Process

5. Work through and redefine the process, identifying areas that can be improved upon quickly at a minimal cost. Ask your employees what prevents them from doing business

effectively and what improvements they have identified (See DESIGN THINKING PROCESSES). Go through each step of the process and ask:

- What is the required output of the process?
- How can the customer's experience be improved?
- How can you add further value to your customers?
- How can you improve your products and services?
- How can you improve integration with suppliers and other strategic partners?
- How can you improve your forecasting?
- How can you run the process more efficiently and effectively?
- How can you leverage technology to improve your process?
- How can you reduce internal organizational conflicts?
- How can you reduce the number of meetings?
- How can you reduce unstructured communication (emails, memos, announcements)?
- How can you reduce time and costs?
- How can you improve your employees' skills and expertise?
- How can your processes be more flexible to meet changing demands and circumstances?
- How can you reduce bureaucracy?

6. Review your redesigned process.

Ask:

- Will the process work as intended?

- How will you measure performance?

- What adjustments are needed to implement the process?

- Will the process conflict with any other process in your organization (for example, a reward program)?

- How will the process integrate into your organization's structure and reporting lines?

7. Implement these ideas.

PROCESS DEFINITION

When defining processes, start by defining a template that you can use for all processes. This template could contain:

- The name of the process.

- An overview of the process, including what it aims to achieve, where it starts and ends, inputs and outputs, what is included in the process, and what is not.

Ask:

- What are the inputs or triggers to start the process?

- What are the results or outputs of the process? Where do the outputs go?

- What are the steps (or tasks) of the process? You might want to use a flow diagram using standard shapes for the start and end, steps, decisions, documents, inputs and outputs, links, and connectors.

- How will exceptions be handled?

- What are the roles and responsibilities?

- What are the controls and authorities?

- How do performance measurement and process verification work?

- What are the process approvals, and how do you plan to keep track of changes to the process?

DESIGN THINKING PROCESSES

There are two core processes that have a significant but often hidden impact on any organization – the *financial processes* and the *reward system*. Both processes tend toward being analytical with an unintended consequence of stifling intuitive thinking, which, in turn, can have an impact on the long-term sustainability of the organization.

FINANCIAL CONTROLS

Financial planning, budgeting, and budget management use the past to predict the future. Targets set for managers serve to attain short-term results but can stifle intuitive thinking. The creative process relies on breakthrough thinking, which is something that cannot be predicted. Stifling intuitive thinking can have long-term impacts when the organization and its products fail to evolve in line with customer needs.

Financial planning for design thinking elements of the business should consist of goals and spending limits. Goals define the breakthrough that the organization wants to achieve. Spending limits reflect the financial reality of the organization.

REWARD SYSTEM

Reward systems are typically designed around achieving financial or performance targets within a set period. Such targets, designed around an organization's fiscal year, are not motivators for design thinking people, whose core motivator is having designed a solution to a huge problem. Breakthrough thinking might not coincide with the financial year and standard reward system periods. Reward systems for design people, therefore, need to be different from those used elsewhere in the organization.

MANAGER'S WORKLOAD

In the module on Structure, we explored the concept that a managers' prime role is to fight fires and to adapt processes for changing circumstances. This is only possible if the manager's time is freed up to focus on problem-solving. Ask your managers to review their current workload. Ask whether the work is routine and whether it follows a set of rules, no matter how complex. If the manager answers yes, then part or all of such work can be automated or delegated to a more junior person.

WORKING CAPITAL REVIEW

The aim of working capital management is to optimize performance while limiting the funds reserved for working capital. The following questions will help you to review the policies and practices that drive your working capital balances.

INVENTORY MANAGEMENT

The objective of *Inventory* (finished goods, work in progress, and raw materials) *management* is to maximize performance demands and to minimize inventory holding.

- Can you improve your demand forecasting to reduce inventory holdings?

- Can you improve your operation's efficiencies and reduce raw materials usage?

- Can you improve communications with your suppliers re your requirements?

- Get competitive quotes for all suppliers. Use these either to renegotiate with your current suppliers or to find new ones.

- Can you improve your stock items to meet increasing demand and reduce investment? Undertake an inventory Pareto analysis (See *PARETO ANALYSIS*). Are you stocking the right inventory items? Can you outsource your slow-moving stock effectively to your suppliers?

- Can you improve your distribution efficiency?

- Is there any obsolete inventory which you can divest?

ACCOUNTS RECEIVABLE

Accounts receivable balances customer satisfaction by providing credit, keeping the organization's cash flows positive, and minimizing bad debts.

- Do you manage outstanding and problematic accounts actively?

- How effective is your credit management process and the monitoring thereof?

- Can you renegotiate more attractive business terms?

- Are there segments of your market that do not require credit terms? Can you refocus your organization to supply these segments?

ACCOUNTS PAYABLE

The objective of *accounts payable* is to balance the delaying of making payments to suppliers with the receiving of funds from customers after goods have been sold. This includes taking advantage of supplier settlement discounts.

- Can you extend your payment terms with your existing supplier base?

- Can you take advantage of settlement discounts? Is it cost-effective to do so?

- Ask for competitive quotes from all your service providers. Use the information either to renegotiate with your current service providers or to find new ones.

PARETO ANALYSIS

The Pareto Principle (also known as the 80/20 rule) states that 20% of the work generates 80% of the results. Joseph Juran named the principle after Vilfredo Pareto, whose research first identified the concept. A Pareto analysis – also known as an ABC analysis – is a widely used principle that applies to almost anything, for example, that:

- 80% of revenue derives from 20% of customers.

- 20% of products or services account for 80% of revenue or profit.

- 80% of complaints arise from 20% of products or services.

- 20% of possible causes of delay account for 80% of actual delays.

- 20% of your sales force accounts for 80% of your sales.

A Pareto analysis provides information that helps you to make decisions. However, it does not cover all areas that might impact an issue. For example, inventory holdings are the result of many factors, including lead times, shipping and handling, product quality, order qualities, and production runs. These factors need to be identified and considered before making any final decisions.

A Pareto analysis can be used to help improve your business performance. While there are many applications of the concept, the examples given will focus on sales and inventory.

DOING A PARETO ANALYSIS

1. Start by identifying what you want to analyze. For example:

    a. Revenue: Which are your most profitable customers?

    b. Inventory: What product items should you have in inventory?

2. Collate the information you require:

    a. Revenue: Gross profit by customer for a year.

    b. Inventory: Sales value by product for a year.

    c. Depending on the volume of information, you might need to do some initial sifting of information. For example, your first inventory analysis might be by product line rather than by product.

3. Manipulate your data:

    a. Capture your data into a spreadsheet.

    b. State each line item as a percentage of the total (for example, product revenue as a percentage of total revenue, and gross profit by customer as a percentage of total gross profit).

    c. Sort your data on these percentages from highest to lowest.

    d. Have a column that accumulates these percentages into a running total. For example, the running total for the first line total will equal the line percentage. The second line running total will add the total from the first line to the percentage of the second line, and so on. The last line item of the running total should be 100%.

    e. Segment your spreadsheet into three. The segment division is where the running total equals 80% and 95%. You will now have three groupings: 0% – 80%, 80% –95%, and 95% – 100%. You might need to adjust these percentages slightly to, for example: 0% – 70%, 70% – 95%, 95% – 100%. You are aiming for:

        i.   20% of your analysis (customers or product) accounting for 80% of the result (gross profit or sales value). These become your "A" customers or product.

        ii. The next 30% (customers or product) accounting for 15% of the result (gross profit or sales value). These become your "B" customers or product.

iii. The final 50% (customers or product) accounting for 5% of the result (gross profit or sales value). These become your "C" customers or product.

Now, interpret the results:

SALES ANALYSIS

In this analysis, you looked at gross profit by customer. The results will have identified your customers in three categories:

- "A" category customers, comprising approximately 20% of your customers but accounting for 80% of your gross profit.

- "B" category customers, comprising approximately 30% of your customers but accounting for 15% of your gross profit.

- "C" category customers, comprising approximately 50% of your customers but accounting for 5% of your gross profit.

You can now develop strategies to manage each of your customer categories. For example:

- "A" customers: consider focusing the majority of your customer partnering efforts on these customers.

- "B" customers: ask how you can convert them to "A" customers. Do you have different service levels for your "B" customers? You might treat them differently to your "A" customers.

- "C" customers: Why do you want them as customers? How can you increase your prices to them?

- Be careful; there might be "B" or "C" customers that order large product volumes. These customers might enable you to negotiate lower volume prices from your suppliers. Identify and manage your strategic customers after considering all facts.

INVENTORY ANALYSIS

With inventory, you looked at sales value by product. The results will have segmented your products into three categories:

- "A" category products, comprising approximately 20% of your product but accounting for 80% of your revenue.

- "B" category products, comprising approximately 30% of your product but accounting for 15% of your revenue.

- "C" category products, comprising approximately 50% of your product but accounting for 5% of your revenue.

You can now use this information to decide on inventory strategies and product stockholding levels.

Start by reviewing your current inventory. It is more than likely that the majority of your inventory by product value will be either in categories "B" or "C", while the majority of your out-of-stock items will be from "A" category items. The implication of this is that you will not have stock immediately on hand to meet demand, resulting in customer frustration and the possibility of lost sales. You will also realize that you have money tied up in inventory that does not contribute to a large proportion of your sales.

You can now develop strategies on how you stock different categories of product:

- "A" products are those that you should always have on hand. How can you replenish these inventory levels frequently to ensure that you always have product on hand while limiting the financial implications of holding such inventory? Are you generating sufficient gross profit from these products?

- "B" products are those items that you either want to have very low levels of inventory or no stock at all. How do you get your supplier to stock these items for you? How do you fulfill customer orders with limited time delays, possibly at higher delivery costs? How do you reduce excessive stock levels quickly to free up cash reserves? Can you charge higher prices for these items?

- "C" products are those you don't want to have in stock at all. Should you even sell these products? How can you reduce or eliminate your inventory levels quickly of these items? Can you charge higher prices for these items?

- Some of your "B" and "C" items could be strategic, requiring you to keep limited inventory levels of these products.

Stocking and ordering levels is a science on its own and is not covered by this tool.

TWO-WAY PARETO ANALYSIS

It is possible to undertake a Pareto analysis in more than one dimension, for example, with one dimension looking at sales volume and the other at sales contribution. The process is described below using an example where we assume that there are five product groupings or categories (numbered 1 through 5) and that a Pareto analysis has been done on both *sales volume* and *contribution*. The analysis resulted in three groupings for each sales volume and contribution (categorized as A, B, and C). The results of the two Pareto analyses are mapped in the diagram below:

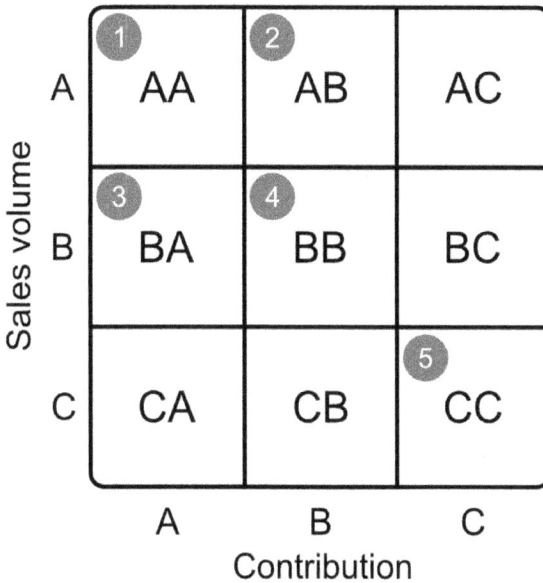

A Two-way Pareto Analysis

We can interpret the results as follows:

- Product 1 falls into the AA quadrant for both volume and contribution. These are major sellers and contribute the majority of your profit. We need to look after these products because they might be the subject of competitive interest. While protecting our position, how do we exploit our competitive advantage?

- Product 2 is an A for volume and a B for contribution. Can we increase margins? What can be done to the product to justify increased margins?

- Product 3 is an excellent contributor (A) but a medium seller (B). Is it subject to competition, and does it need protection? How can sales volumes be increased?

- Product 4 is mediocre under both measures. How can sales volumes be increased? Does it need repositioning? Does it need replacing? Does it need funding to move it toward the AA block?

- Product 5 should be phased out unless there is a strategic reason for keeping it (for example, it may be a new product, or it might be essential to another product). While always looking to eliminate these products, beware of the type of organization you are in. If, for example, you sell bicycles, you might need several slow sellers to attract customers as part of your strategic positioning. Your customers come to your store because they know they will always find what they want.

CONTINUOUS IMPROVEMENT

While implementing improvements to your organization, do so within the context of continuous improvement. In reviewing your organization's performance, ask:

- What quality management systems do we have in place?
- Are they aimed at improving the customer's experience?
- Do they cover all aspects of the organization's operations?
- Do employees embrace quality management?
- What can be done to improve quality management?

Some of the practices to help achieve continuous improvement are listed below, with a brief introduction to each. It is beyond the scope of the tool to provide details on how to implement each of these approaches.

BENCHMARKING

Benchmarking consists of comparing your results against yardsticks. These yardsticks could be based on historical performance, competitor performance, or against best-in-class within or external to your industry.

In doing an external comparison, ask why these entities are successful in achieving these benchmarks.

TOTAL QUALITY MANAGEMENT (TQM)

TQM focuses on designing and delivering quality products to customers. It is a culture embracing a total commitment to quality and everybody's involvement in continuous improvement.

The core principles of TQM are:

- Commitment to quality. The workforce is committed to delivering quality products, the individual is committed to the customer, management is committed to TQM, and everyone, including the organization's suppliers, is committed to quality as a whole.

- Scientific tools, technologies, and methods are used to assist managers in making systematic changes to processes and products.

- Total involvement in quality through teamwork and empowerment.

- Continuous improvement. Something must be improved every day, and improvement should be never-ending.

SIX SIGMA

The Six Sigma approach is a set of management techniques intended to improve business processes by greatly reducing the probability of an error or defect. It is a rigorous and analytical approach to quality and continuous improvement. The objective is to improve profits through defect reduction, yielding improved customer satisfaction and best-in-class performance. It is often considered an improvement over TQM. It consists of five steps: define, measure, analyze, improve and control.

- **Definition** is about determining the problem and narrowing the scope to achieve measurable goals within a few months. Teams are established to solve the problem.

- **Measurement** is the gathering of data for high-level analysis.

- **Analysis** includes observations as to why the problem has arisen, often owing to people-related issues.

- **Improvement** comes from recommendations and implementation thereof.

- **Control** is the final stage. The team creates controls to ensure the sustainability of the solution.

BUSINESS PROCESS REENGINEERING (BPR)

BPR helps an organization to create value for customers by eliminating barriers that create distance between employees and customers. The focus is reviewing and redesigning processes to provide the best quality goods and services at the lowest cost. The primary focus is always on meeting customer needs.

AGILE

Agile is the ability to quickly adapt to succeed in uncertain and turbulent times. It's about having an approach to understanding what is going on in your operating environment, identifying the uncertainty you are facing, and working out how you will respond and adapt as you go along. It is about capturing opportunities as they develop, quicker than your competitors.

Agile teams are small, flexible, cross-functional teams working on innovation projects. Typically, they are self-steering, enjoy freedom from the controls and constraints characteristic of many organizations. Their aim is to speed up work whilst improving team motivation.

Once initial teams are successful, the agile team concept is expanded throughout the organization until it becomes an ingrained approach to tackling uncertainty.

The agile concept has been used extensively in software development to break the long lead times associated with other approaches. The agile approach is different primarily in how it focuses on people and how they work together. Solutions evolve through collaboration between self-organizing cross-functional teams.

SURVIVING THE CLIMATE CRISIS

"Firms ignoring climate crisis will go bankrupt!"

*Mark Carney, Governor of The Bank of England (*Article heading from
The Guardian 13 Oct 2019)

No matter your views on what causes climate change, we all saw a different world during the Covid-19 pandemic lockdowns. We saw clean air in some of the most polluted cities in the world, we saw clean rivers, and we saw wild animals entering urban areas. We saw the potential for a better world. We have also seen the devastation we as humans have had on the natural environment throughout the world.

The pandemic initially appeared to put a hold on many of the calls for mitigating the major environmental concerns, but these appear to be coming back with renewed vigor. For example, Air France has had stringent conditions included in their bailout package aimed at reducing their carbon emissions.

Organizations are going to face increasing pressures from multiple stakeholders to reduce their impact on the environment. Get ahead of the game and initiate a program to monitor and mitigate your organization's impacts.

The following process may help you in improving your environmental impact:

STEP 1: COMMIT

A journey to ongoing environmental impact limitation is a long-term commitment and will require ongoing championing by the CEO or business owner. There are three legs to this commitment: *Compliance, Improvement,* and *Prevention.* Before committing:

- Understand why you are doing this. Is it because of stakeholder pressures? Legislative requirements? Changes in competition? Your personal sense of environmental responsibility? You will need a strong motivator for the journey you are undertaking to remind you why you are initiating these changes, especially when times get tough.

- Do some research into environmental challenges. What is climate change? Is this the only environmental issue? Is it the most important challenge? What are the biggest challenges relevant to your industry? What is the truth, and what is fake news?

- What international environmental standards (for example, ISO 14001) might you want to comply with? What is the compelling reason for you to comply with such standards?

- What is your personal stance? Will it hinder or help with your organization's journey to improving its environmental impact?

- How will you sustain your commitment to reducing your environmental impact in the future? What will get in the way? What do you need to do to maintain momentum?

- Summarize your findings and ask yourself, "Is this what I want for the organization?"

- If yes, write a commitment statement. You will use this statement to communicate why you are taking your organization in this direction, driving the reason for the change initiative required to implement your commitment.

STEP 2: REVIEW

You have committed to reducing your impact on the environment. Now you need to determine what impacts your organization has on the environment. Depending on your organization, this could be a substantial undertaking.

You could review your entire organization's impacts yourself, have an internal team do it, or appoint an outside organization specializing in the area. If you keep it in-house:

- Do a review of your environmental impacts.

- Focus on your most obvious and major impacts. Once you have these priorities sorted, go back to your list of priorities to determine which areas to tackle next.

- Establish and empower teams to tackle each area. Your teams must have the ability, enthusiasm, and authority to review the organization, make recommendations, and implement them.

Whatever approach you decide on, you will need a substantial effort to review your organization's environmental impacts. Much of the review could overlap with a review of the organization's operational efficiencies as a whole. Don't waste this opportunity to review your organization by restricting your review to environmental impacts. At the same time, avoid losing sight of the end objective by making the review too large. You still have an organization to run.

You need a formal process to ensure that all areas are identified and reviewed, and where information is collected. This will help to ensure that sufficient information is available later in the process when deciding on which initiatives to prioritize. The objective would be to ensure that someone not involved in the review can quickly pick up on the work done.

As a minimum, you will require:

- The area or problem being covered. For example, the area of operations or the type of environmental issue.

- A more detailed description of the area and current status, including measures and results, awareness, and legislation requirements.

- Any key findings from the review.

- Any conclusions reached.

- Recommended actions to mitigate any problem identified. This would include inputs to the prioritization process, including:

  - An estimate of how effective the recommended mitigation approach will be in reducing the environmental problem identified.

  - Any impact that the recommended mitigation could have on the organization. This could be positive, neutral, or negative.

  - The estimated cost of such mitigation.

  - The duration to implement the mitigation strategy.

- Any other comments or additional information or supporting documentation.

These reviews would need to be easily assessable for future use and referral.

This review has been divided into three areas: *Strategy and Culture*, *Operations*, and *Employees and Community*.

Strategy and culture

Your strategy and culture might unintentionally encourage practices that go against your commitment to reducing your environmental impact. Review the following to ensure that these practices are not going to hinder your initiative:

- Review your strategy to make sure there are no aspects that could encourage negative impacts. If appropriate, change your strategy to include your commitment to changing your environmental impact.

- Review your values to make sure they contribute to that which you want to achieve.

- Question your culture. Is the organization's culture one that encourages responsible stewardship of the environment?

- Review your leadership style. Do you encourage a responsible organization?

- Review your measurement and reward systems to ensure that they encourage environmental responsibility.

Operations

Your operations are most likely your greatest area of impact. Review your operations by identifying and evaluating their impacts.

Identifying impacts

- Which of your operations and activities could have an environmental impact?

- What materials, resources, and energy sources are used by your operations?

- What emissions are there (air, water, or land)?

- What waste or scrap is generated? Does its disposal impact the environment?

- How could your products and services impact the environment (including packaging, use, end-of-life disposal)?

- Does your land or infrastructure impact the environment?

- Which of your materials handling or storage activities could lead to accidental releases?

Evaluating impacts

- Are the identified impacts actual or potential?

- Are the impacts beneficial or damaging to the environment? What parts of the environment do they affect?

- What is the extent and duration of these impacts?

- What is the frequency of these impacts?

- What is the likelihood of these impacts happening?

- What regulations exist to govern the impact?

- Have interested parties expressed concern about any of these impacts?

Employees and community

Your employees impact the environment when commuting to and from work and in their lives outside of work. Your workplace is situated within a community, and your organization and its people have an impact on that community. Consider initiatives that could either reduce the impact your employees have on the environment or improve your community. These could include:

- Asking how you can reduce the impacts of your employees commuting to work (for example, working remotely, carpooling, providing transport).

- Introducing information awareness initiatives, explaining how your employees can lessen their environmental impact outside the workplace.

- Initiate, be involved in, or support community initiatives, either surrounding your place of work or where your employees live.

STEP 3: PLANS

You will have multiple recommendations and plans as a result of the review. Some of them will be easy to implement and can be done immediately. Others will require time and resources.

Simple solutions can be misleading. I remember early on in my career wanting to implement a paper recycling process at my workplace. With great enthusiasm, I placed special recycling bins around the offices. The initiative had limited results for two reasons:

1. I had not fully investigated what would happen to the paper once the bins were full. In those days, there was no separate collection process for waste paper. Paper recycling required engaging with a separate company for collection and recycling, which required engaging with my firm's bureaucracy.

2. I had not engaged with my fellow workers to ask for their commitment to my paper recycling initiative.

Capture and consolidate all recommendations and the plans for implementation in a project management tool. This will help you keep track of your environmental impact reduction journey, prioritize initiatives to allocate limited resources, and report on progress made.

STEP 4: PRIORITIZE

Some projects will need to be implemented no matter what, for example, to meet legislative requirements. Such projects will reduce your capacity and resources to implement other initiatives. This process will help you to prioritize the remaining projects.

Begin by defining a number of criteria against which you are going to evaluate each initiative or plan identified, and prioritize their implementation. Such criteria and their means of measurement could include:

- Possible effectiveness in reducing your impact on the environment (rated *high/medium/low*).

- Possible impact on the current organization (rated *positive/ neutral/negative*).

- Possible cost of the initiative (rated *high/medium/low*).

- Possible duration of the initiative (rated *within three months/ within a year/longer*).

Define what each of the criteria you have selected means to you and the values of each measurement range (either a percentage change or in dollar terms).

Take your list of projects identified earlier in the process and score them against these criteria. Convert the scores to a number and add up the scores. Allocate priorities against a range of scores. For example, there are four criteria listed above. The scoring for each criterion would be 3 for the highest, 2 for the middle option, with 1 being the lowest score. The highest score possible would be 12 and the lowest 4. You could then say that any project scoring between 10 and 12 would be an *A priority*, scoring between 7 and 9 would be a *B priority*, and below 7 would be a *C priority*, with your minimum score being 4. Don't feel obliged to rely exclusively on the scoring. Review each project and adjust its priority based on your intuition and knowledge.

You might have a limited budget, which will require reducing your list further. Take your A projects and order them from highest priority downwards. Add up the total cost estimate of each project on an accumulative basis until you have met your budget. The projects that fall within budget are those that you will focus on during the current financial year. Projects that don't make the cut will have to wait for budget increases.

STEP 5: IMPLEMENT

You have plans that can be implemented. Change management will be critical in ensuring changed behavior from your employees and the success of your efforts.

STEP 6: COMMUNICATE

You have done all the hard work to reduce your environmental impacts. When you started the process, you defined why you needed to do this. Now you need to inform all your stakeholders about what you have achieved. This might include:

- Giving customers an additional reason for continuing to buy from you.

- Motivating and inspiring employees by reminding them that they are working for and contributing to a great organization.

- Demonstrating to investors that you are continually evolving and improving while being responsible citizens.

- Showing local communities that you are making an effort to improve the environment.

STEP 7: COMPLIANCE

This step consists of ensuring ongoing compliance with your commitment to reducing your environmental impact. It could take a number of forms, including:

- Ongoing monitoring of performance through your management performance process.
- Ongoing reviews to identify further areas for improvement.
- Monitoring and returns to meet legislated requirements, including formal compliance audits.

8.3 Measuring Your Performance

AWARENESS

Key performance indicators (KPIs) measure performance on an ongoing basis. KPIs and performance information are captured and collated in a management information system.

Good KPIs:

- Provide an objective way to track the performance and success of your strategy.
- Provide a measure of performance change over time.
- Focus attention on what really matters to succeed.
- Allow for the measurement of results rather than just the work performed.
- Provide a common understanding of what you are trying to achieve.

- Help reduce the uncertainties typically found in strategies.

Creating a balance of measures across your organization is essential. With this in mind, Robert Kaplan and David Norton developed the *Balanced Scorecard*[25]. In essence, the balanced scorecard looks to measure:

- Financial performance: the financial results we are aiming for.

- Customers' and other stakeholders' performance: what customers and other stakeholders expect from an organization.

- The performance of internal processes: the processes in which the organization needs to excel.

- Organizational capacity: what we need to invest in today for future success (human capital, infrastructure, technology, culture, and other capabilities).

Guiding principles for defining KPIs:

- Are the KPIs balanced across all critical areas of the organization?

- To what extent are the KPIs aligned with the strategy in terms of your business and customer focus?

  - Business focus, for example, product, customer, technology, production capability, and distribution.

  - Customer value proposition, for example, low costs, quality, speed, service, and innovation.

- To what extent will the KPIs last over time?

- To what extent are the KPIs aimed at making the whole more than the parts?

---

25 Robert S. Kaplan and David P. Norton. The Balanced Scorecard: Translating Strategy into Action. Boston: Harvard Business School Press, 1996.

When defining your KPIs, keep the concept of the triple bottom line – financial performance, social performance, and environmental performance – in mind.

ACTION

The following actions will help to improve measuring your performance:

Defining KPIs

- List your information needs as follows:
  - The information required to manage customer needs.
  - The information required to help land new customers and keep track of the sales pipeline.
  - All key management decisions made on an ongoing basis by all employees, including expenditure priorities, pricing decisions, and employee effort.
  - Other information required to ensure the effective monitoring of all aspects of the organization.
  - Examine the income statement and balance sheet. What further information is needed in particular to manage large value items?
  - Ask your key staff for their information needs.
  - Search the internet for KPIs specific to your industry.
- Identify your KPIs in line with your strategy.
- Make sure all aspects of the balanced scorecard are covered in your identified KPIs.
- Review the KPIs to ensure that they will drive the desired behavior.

- Select the KPIs that will help manage the organization best.

- Determine how often you need to track the KPIs. The duration of tracking will depend on your operating circumstances. You might need to track certain of your KPIs in real time, and others daily, weekly, or monthly.

- Determine how to collect the supporting information for the KPIs.

- Determine what systems are necessary to collect the information. Consider using manual methods such as flip charts to collect and display performance information. Aim at having measures in place quickly and at a low cost.

- Regularly review your KPIs to ensure they are driving the desired behavior. Make sure the KPI is measuring an outcome and that you are not measuring something purely for the sake of measurement. In particular, ask if any of your measures restrict (rather than encourage) design thinking.

Tracking performance

- Regularly track performance trends and interpret them. (See *SALES INTERVENTIONS* and *DECLINE AND TURNAROUND*)

- Ensure that you have early warning systems in place to track changes in competitor behavior. Look out for changes in the marketplace, too, such as the emergence of disruptive technologies.

- Review your processes, strategies, and the marketplace to determine where you are vulnerable, and then take corrective action.

SALES INTERVENTIONS

At the first sign of a downturn in sales or competitor hostile activity, treat the threat as a priority by:

- Finding out what is really happening.

- Considering your options carefully.

- Taking swift action.

- Monitoring the effects of your interventions.

- Continuing to monitor and react until the emergency is over.

- Not letting your competitors know you are hurting!

FALLING SALES

When you have falling sales, you need to act quickly:

- Forecast your cash flow in light of the falling sales and take appropriate action to remain cash positive.

- Perform a sales break-even analysis to calculate your bottom sales level before you go into loss. This will help determine the severity of the situation.

- Try to understand what caused the decline in sales. Don't overreact. Think of all the possible consequences before taking action.

- Determine where you can cut costs, especially in terms of your overheads. Consider putting capital projects on hold. If the sales downtrend is severe, you will have to act quickly to save your organization.

- Look at how you can increase sales by:

- Seeking customers: Are you generating sufficient leads from advertising, networking, and promotions? Why not? Do you ask your new customers how they heard about you?

- Stimulating customer interest: Are your products and services appropriate for the market? Do customers realize precisely what you are selling? Conduct an objective review of your products and services and compare them with those of your competitors.

- Satisfying customer needs: Why are customers not buying? Review your product marketing mix. Is it still relevant? How can you change it?

- Selling: Are your sales techniques working? Do you need to retrain your sales force?

■ Keep your bank informed of the situation, especially if you have an overdraft facility.

■ Continue paying your creditors, especially your suppliers and particularly your *strategic* suppliers. Consider asking for extended payment terms where possible.

STAGNANT SALES

Stagnant sales generally indicate that an organization could be heading toward failure. In this case, there is usually enough time to react. Take action with these steps:

■ Continue implementing your marketing plan.

■ Determine the causes of your stagnation.

■ Review your marketing strategies and plans in light of your findings as to why your organization is stagnating.

■ Look at diversifying by reviewing your:

- Products or services: what can you do to revitalize them? What additional markets are there for them?

- Customers: what new customers can you attract?

- New markets: what other markets can you serve?

- Make sure you are not the problem. A stagnating organization is often because the owner is complacent and unwilling to adapt to developments in the market.

RAPID GROWTH

Rapidly growing demand for your products or services creates challenges of its own. One of the biggest challenges in a growth scenario is funding such growth – you need to purchase more inventory, employ more staff, possibly fund a larger credit book, and potentially increase capital expenditure. A further challenge is how your processes and systems will cope with the increased demand. Mitigate this by:

- Undertaking regular cash flow forecasts to fully understand your situation.

- Making sure the increased demand is sustainable before committing to long-term costs.

- Talking to your bank about your increased funding needs. You will need a good track record with your bank, financial records showing the increase in demand, financial forecasts, and strong financial controls to be in place.

- Looking at the scalability of your processes and procedures. How well will your systems react to increased sales? Addressing this is something you can do relatively quickly and in advance of any increased sales volumes.

- Considering strategies other than internal growth:

- If your local laws allow it, appoint contractor employees rather than full-time employees. Consider using sub-contractors and outsourcing various functions.

- Find new partners or directors for your organization. Be careful not to rush this process as there can be long-lasting (negative) consequences. Make sure of their fit in your organization as well as their capabilities and health. Obtain legal and tax advice in terms of how best to structure any agreements with new partners.

- Can you franchise your organization to meet the market demand for your products or services? Get expert advice before you commit fully to this approach.

- Consider a merger or acquisition with one of your competitors. Get expert advice before you commit fully to this.

- Licensing your products or services to existing companies is an effective strategy, especially for new markets (for example, overseas). The licensee will pay you a royalty. Get legal and tax advice before committing to this process.

COMPETITOR AGGRESSION

Competitors are always a potential threat to any organization. Your marketing strategy should include a review of competitors. If you have a significant competitor, it might be best to have a strategy to stay under the radar and avoid taking them on directly. Rather find niches in which you can operate successfully. Let them think you are insignificant.

Keep an eye on your competitors. Look for warning signs that they may become more aggressive. Such signs include new senior management, moving to larger premises, acquiring another organization (or being acquired), recruiting new sales staff, raising capital, or launching new products or services.

There are several tactics that an aggressive competitor might employ. These include:

- **Starting a Price War**

Make sure your overall differentiating strategy does not depend entirely on price. Focus on where your customers see you adding value. Continue providing this service with a bit more effort to negate the effects of the price war. If you do need to drop your prices, either meet your competitor's price or go in slightly higher. Don't encourage further price drops by cutting your prices below those of your competitors.

- **Misinformation**

It would be best if you counteracted any misinformation campaigns by stating the truth. You can be defensive and set the record straight, or you can be aggressive by showing how your competitor's products and services are inferior. Beware of the legal implications of such an approach. Your best plan is to ensure that you have excellent working partnerships with your customers so that they know when misinformation is being spread.

- **Stealing Customers**

Stay close to your customers and become their business partners. Continually look for new customers.

- **Stealing Your Staff**

Staff turnover is a reality of doing business. You can reduce staff turnover by making the work environment more attractive than that of your competitors and by rewarding key staff. Make it unattractive for key personnel to move. It is wise that you plan for the eventuality of staff leaving you. Ensure that key staff members have a nominated deputy and that the deputies have their knowledge (for example, markets and customers), and, if possible, that this information is captured into a CRM system.

- **Interfering With Your Suppliers**

Supplier interference often happens when a larger competitor puts pressure on joint suppliers, making it difficult for you to trade. Such practices, which are more likely to occur where there is a limited source of suppliers, are less likely but not unknown in distribution networks. Remain close to your suppliers but have a strategy in place to mitigate such hard play. Review your distribution networks to make sure you are not vulnerable.

- **Disruptive Technologies**

Keep abreast of developments and identify disruptive technologies early. If it looks as if the disruptive strategy is here to stay, then embrace the changes. You will, in all likelihood, be required to redesign your operating model, which could mean writing off items like capital equipment. Determine whether it is better to embrace the changes than to go out of business.

- **Legal Proceedings**

Competitors might instigate legal proceedings against you by contesting your trade name, your brand, your logo, or by claiming copyright infringement. Ensure that sure you comply with any legal requirements in advance of facing legal action. Obtain competent legal advice should legal proceedings be initiated.

Adapted from: Peter Hingston's *Effective Marketing*[26]

---

26   Peter Hingston, Effective Marketing. Dorling Kindersley, 2001.

DECLINE AND TURNAROUND

Change is inevitable in any organization. Organizational failure is often a result of the organization's inability to change.

An organization is in decline when performance and operations slow down over an extended period. It is often due to management being slow to react to warning signs and not addressing problems until it is too late.

The sooner you can get into action in a turnaround situation, the more options will be available to you. This means recognizing the tell-tale signs of decline – something much easier said than done!

WARNING SIGNS THAT YOUR ORGANIZATION MIGHT BE IN TROUBLE

Some of the more common signs of decline include:

- Cash flow constraints.
- Increasing debt with further funding being unavailable.
- Constantly in survival mode, with unpaid suppliers, growing inventory, late deliveries, growing outstanding receivables, and an inability to meet debt repayments.
- Deteriorating sales and a diminishing customer base, with a resultant loss in market share.
- Reducing gross or net profitability.
- Market disruptions.
- Inadequate financial and performance record keeping.
- Lack of strategic thinking and planning (or a common understanding of the strategy throughout the organization).

- An increase in staff turnover with the best employees leaving.

- The owner is unable to take a vacation because the organization cannot operate without them.

TURNING IT AROUND

A seven-step approach to organizational turnaround is provided below. While clear steps are shown, there will be overlaps between steps. These steps are not designed around any legislation on bankruptcy or liquidation but will hopefully help you to avoid reaching that stage.

Step 1: Review One's Own Abilities

Your first question to ask is whether you are the correct person to lead the turnaround. Look at yourself honestly and remember that the decline happened under your watch. Realistically, can you lead the change, or do you need to find someone else to head up the organization? A turnaround situation often requires strong, commanding, or even charismatic leadership.

If you decide to bring someone else on board, you can continue working in the organization as long as you are aware of your different (and often conflicting) roles as owner and employee, but not the boss.

Step 2: Analyze the Problem

Many factors contribute to organizational decline. These are often not found in isolation but in combination. It is important to identify these factors, categorize them into internal or external drivers, and focus on them during your turnaround.

- **Internal Factors**

This includes machinery and equipment adequacy, technology capacity, culture, management team capabilities, financial management and control, and employee morale.

When addressing internal factors, you will typically focus on efficiency strategies such as improved financial controls, improved systems, improved marketing efforts, new technologies, and the training and development of staff.

- **External Factors**

This can include changes to competitors, suppliers, disruptive technologies, customer behavior, industry outlook, demographics, the economy, the political environment, the social environment, and environmental changes, including climate change.

Typically, external factors are best addressed with entrepreneurial creativity and innovative strategies.

At the end of the analysis, you *must* be able to determine whether the organization is still viable.

Step 3: Take Control

You must take control of the situation immediately to halt further decline, with your primary objective being to stop the bleeding. Quick action is required in the areas discovered in your analysis. You may want to:

- Take control of your cash: Obtain regular cash flow forecasts – at least weekly. Consider consolidating bank accounts and authorization protocols.

- Tighten up on controls: This could include tightening expenditure authorizations, ordering and releasing inventory, granting credit, collecting debtor balances, and improving site security.

- Assess your current management team: If they got you into your current situation, who can get you out? Who will resist change? Who is stuck so completely in the old way of doing things that they will not change? You might need high-energy performers from outside the organization to effect the required changes.

- Review your budgeting and monitoring processes and decide whether they require improvement.

- Consider changing the organization's culture.

Step 4: Define A Turnaround Strategy

You have identified the causes of your current situation and have started some immediate changes. Now you need to define a comprehensive turnaround strategy. Start with a vision for the organization that incorporates the turnaround. To drive the vision, you will need to change your corporate culture.

Develop a detailed turnaround strategy to address the problems identified in the analysis. Use this strategy to guide your detailed plans and sell the turnaround to your stakeholders. It is a vital step in the turnaround process, so don't skimp on this exercise!

Your strategy could include:

- The objectives of the turnaround.
- Any envisaged impacts on products or services.
- A marketing plan.
- An estimate on the market potential and its competitors.
- The management team, their experience, and changes to the team.
- Sourcing or manufacturing of products and services.

- An operations plan.
- Projected financial results and a comparison of where you would be without a turnaround strategy.
- Financial requirements and how the money will be used.
- The anticipated return on investment (ROI) for investors.

You will need to start communicating with key stakeholders. These could include key personnel, the board of directors, employees and unions, customers, vendors and distributors, banks, and anyone else you pay regularly.

Some examples of turnaround strategies are included in the *TURNAROUND STRATEGIES* box below.

Step 5: Detailed Planning

Now that you have a turnaround strategy that your various stakeholders have bought into, it's time to do detailed planning to make the strategy a reality and the turnaround a success.

Break each of your various strategies down into action plans. Look for linkages between activities – for example, a task that can only be done when another is complete. Set responsibilities and timelines. Ask for input from key employees and your board of directors, and re-plan if necessary.

Capture your plans in a project management tool.

Step 6: Implement Your Plans

Implementing plans is not only about systematically ensuring that the plans are delivered on time. It is also about continuously interacting with people. Your employees will need your ongoing support and mentoring. You need to motivate your employees and boost their morale continually. They must believe in the new vision for the organization and that the turnaround strategies will work.

You also need to assure your critical stakeholders (customers, vendors, suppliers, financiers, shareholders) that your turnaround strategy is working and that you will be open for business well into the future.

Step 7: Continuous Review

Continuously reviewing your progress is about ongoing tracking, monitoring, and controlling. It ensures the organization's ongoing performance and determines the effectiveness of the turnaround interventions and strategies. This can only be achieved once you have defined your critical key performance indicators. Depending on your results, you might need to adjust your turnaround plans.

Adapted from Stuart Slatter's *Corporate Recovery: A Guide to Turnabout Management.*[27]

TURNAROUND STRATEGIES

Several turnaround strategy ideas and examples are listed, based on different scenarios. The list is not exclusive.

ASSET REDUCTION STRATEGIES

1. Divest your organization of operating units

2. Consider a management buy-out

3. Divest your organization of specific assets

---

27   Stuart Slatter, Corporate Recovery: A Guide to Turnabout Management, Penguin Business, 1984.

4. Review alternative financial options such as sale and leaseback

5. Reduce working capital:
   a. Inventory
      o Stop purchasing
      o Cancel outstanding orders
      o Return goods to suppliers
      o Order more frequently
      o Change suppliers
      o Sell surplus raw materials to third parties
      o Get rid of slow-moving or obsolete stock
   b. Reduce debtors
      o Identify overdue accounts and stop supplying those customers
      o Contact your customers and reassure them of your continued business
      o Tighten up on credit analysis
      o Consider financing your debtors book
      o Change your settlement terms, including offering a discount for immediate settlement
   c. Creditors
      o Determine whether and how you can extend payment terms

COST-REDUCTION STRATEGIES

1. Reduce material costs
   a. Improve buying practices
   b. Utilize material better
   c. Use different materials

2. Reduce labor unit costs

    a. Increase productivity

        o Ensure that the management style of all managers is relevant to productivity enhancement

        o Change the organizational structure

        o Offer incentive payments

        o Change production methods

        o Change recruitment, selection, and training

    b. Reduce total labor costs

        o Don't hire new employees to replace resignations

        o Early retirement

        o Voluntary retrenchment

        o Cut out or reduce overtime

        o Reschedule paid vacation

        o Reschedule work

        o Reduce the hours in the work week

        o Cut wages, salaries, and bonuses

        o Freeze increases

        o Transfer employees elsewhere in the organization

        o Retrench: if you need to retrench, do it once and do it deeply but not to the bone

3. Reduce overheads (manufacturing, marketing, distribution, travel, training, support, administration)

4. Restructure debt

REVENUE-GENERATING STRATEGIES

1. Marketing-improvement strategy

    • Marketing and selling processes

    • Staff morale

    • Change prices

- Focus on a small number of products and a small number of customers
- Improve selling effort
- Rationalize the product or service line
- Redirect promotion efforts

2. Change products or services to meet a changing market

3. Acquisition

Adapted from Stuart Slatter's *Corporate Recovery: A Guide to Turnabout Management*

9

Corporate Governance

Corporate governance is the practice by which organizations are kept accountable to:

- Protect the assets and resources of the organization;
- Hold senior management accountable for their decisions and actions.

It includes ensuring that checks and balances are in place to decrease the abuse of power, increase the integrity of decision-making, and ensure greater transparency through openness and accountability.

Corporate governance aims to:

- Protect shareholder rights and encourage investment.
- Encourage ethical leadership and corporate citizenship.
- Ensure compliance with legal and regulatory obligations.

- Ensure that risks are identified and managed.
- Hold the organization accountable to the broader society in which it operates.

As an organization grows, good corporate governance becomes an increasingly important factor. You need only look at large listed organizations that have collapsed through unethical behavior to see the importance of good corporate governance.

Effective corporate governance starts early in an organization's life and is an excellent way of obtaining ongoing, impartial advice from a group of people who support the owner's endeavors. Introducing corporate governance is a continuum. A start-up organization might initially have limited governance structures. As the organization grows, further governance structures and practices can be introduced.

The main participants in corporate governance consist of the:

- **Shareholders**
  The shareholders elect the board of directors to protect their interests.

- **Board of Directors**
  The board of directors oversees corporate performance and appoints the CEO for the day-to-day running of the organization. The board often operates by appointing a number of select committees, including an **audit** committee (internal controls, financial systems reliability, and financial reporting), a **governance** committee (effectiveness of governance activities), and a **compensation** committee (policies and compensation packages).

- **CEO**
  The CEO is responsible for strategic planning and execution, performance reporting, and risk management. The CEO

keeps the board informed of ongoing performance and appoints senior managers to help run the organization's day-to-day operations.

- **Senior Managers**
  The senior managers ensure smooth operations by creating and supervising internal processes and controls. They oversee the workability of the structure, a culture of integrity and ethics, and that processes are implemented to avoid and detect misconduct.

- **Stakeholders**
  An organization's stakeholders are either *directly* involved in the organization (employees, customers, and suppliers) or *indirectly* involved (community organizations, lobby, and campaigning groups). They have a direct interest in the well-being and ethical behavior of the organization.

This module looks at three areas of corporate governance in more detail, those being corporate governance practices, financial controls, and risk management.

9.1 Corporate Governance Practices

AWARENESS

Corporate governance consists of a set of processes, procedures, and safeguards by which an organization is directed to protect the interests of its many stakeholders, and covers practically every sphere of the organization. Ultimately, it is about transparent, answerable, and accountable leadership.

The seven characteristics of good corporate governance are discipline, transparency, independence, accountability, responsibility, fairness, and social responsibility.

- **Discipline:** A commitment to the underlying principles of good governance by adhering to behavior that is universally recognized and accepted to be correct and proper through the adherence to procedures, processes, and authority structures established by the organization.
- **Transparency:** The availability of accurate and timely financial and non-financial performance information so that stakeholders can make meaningful analyses of the organization's actions and performance.
- **Independence:** Having mechanisms in place to minimize or avoid potential conflicts of interest, particularly in decision-making. Such mechanisms include internal processes, the independence of the board, and external auditors.
- **Accountability:** Making commitments, taking responsibility for and delivering on commitments, being judged against commitments made, being transparent, and reporting on performance.
- **Responsibility:** Being responsible for personal choices, admitting mistakes and failures, and accepting responsibility for the organization's impact on all stakeholders.
- **Fairness:** All decisions taken and processes implemented must not create an unfair advantage to any one particular party. The rights of various stakeholder groups must be acknowledged and respected.
- **Social responsibility:** Social responsibility is not only about fulfilling legal expectations but also about going beyond what is expected. A good corporate citizen is increasingly seen as one who is non-discriminatory, and non-exploitative,

but who is responsible when it comes to environmental and human rights issues.

ACTION

The following actions will help to improve your governance.

Values and ethics

Ask yourself:

- Do you live by your organization's vision, values, and ethics?
- What do you need to do to improve ethics and governance within your workforce?
- Can you implement an anonymous employee reporting and feedback mechanism?

Governance structures

Ask yourself:

- What governance structures do you want?
- What are the roles and responsibilities within the structures?
- How will you incorporate these structures into the daily running of your organization?

Start small. Appoint an independent person as a board member to act as your advisor. Hold regular meetings with that person to discuss all aspects of organizational performance, strategy, regulatory compliance, social responsibility, risk management, and stakeholder management.

Processes and policies

Ask yourself:

- What do you need to do to improve internal controls and regulatory compliance within your organization?
- What additional policies do you need? For example, codes of ethics and conduct, whistleblowing process, code of corporate governance, environmental impact policy, social impact policy, succession plan, and grievance mechanism.
- Does your strategic planning incorporate good governance?
- Appoint an external financial auditor to review your financial controls and records annually.

Stakeholder communication

What do stakeholders want?

- Employees want job security, job satisfaction, compensation.
- Suppliers want regular payments, continuity of business, long-term relationships.
- Customers want high-quality products/services, good service, value for money.
- Competitors want ethical competition, fair business practices.
- Financial institutions want security on loans, interest.
- Shareholders want a return on their investment and predictable risk.
- The government wants taxes, employment, and community development.

- The community wants social, health, and environmental responsibility, community development, and fair employment.
- The media want transparency and honesty.

In line with the above, determine appropriate communication strategies for all of your organization's stakeholders. The following steps will help you to define your communications strategy:

- Start by identifying the stakeholders (or groups of stakeholders) that will have an impact on (both positive and negative), or be impacted by, the organization's communications.

- For each stakeholder, determine what their interest is in the organization and what will motivate their behavior. Do they have a financial stake or an emotional interest? Are they supporters, or are they against the organization? How will they influence or impact the organization?

- Determine strategies to maximize or minimize the impact of the various stakeholders. This could include active involvement, retaining support, reassurance, or preventing unwelcome surprises.

- Determine the means of communication or management intervention required for each group of stakeholders.

- Determine the frequency of communications or intervention.

- Determine who has the lead responsibility for communicating with each stakeholder group.

- Make communication an ongoing practice.

Decision-making

Ask yourself the following questions before making any major decision:

1. Do I have a conflict of interest that might influence my decision?

2. Do I have all the facts to enable me to make a decision?

3. Have I understood the motivation for the decision and any subsequent discussions?

4. Is the decision-making process transparent to the organization's stakeholders?

5. Is the decision seen as acting responsively and responsibly to all stakeholders?

6. Is the decision in line with good citizenship?

7. Does the decision amount to good stewardship of the organization and its assets?

8. Is this a rational decision based on all the facts?

9. Is the decision in the best interests of the organization?

10. Would I or the organization be embarrassed if the decision or the decision process were published in the media?

11. Have I exercised intellectual honesty?

9.2 Financial Controls

AWARENESS

Growing organizations require cash to continue growing. Financing growth will always be a challenge to small, cash-strapped organizations. Uncontrolled growth and expenditure will put excessive strain on cash flows, with the risk of untimely bankruptcy.

The management of an organization's cash flow is the most critical aspect of financial control. An organization can be profitable but still go into liquidation because of a shortage of cash. Similarly, an organization operating at a loss can continue operating provided it has a positive cash flow. Any organization that collects money before it provides its service or product should not have cash flow problems. Organizations that only collect payment after providing their products or services are more likely to have sales funding challenges.

The primary aim of having financial controls in place should be to stay in business. The elements of financial control include systems and internal controls, management accounts, working capital management, budgeting, KPI reporting, financial management, accounting policies and procedures, year-end audits, and reporting.

ACTION

The following actions will help you to improve your organization's financial controls:

- If your organization is large enough, employ an accountant.

- Make sure that you have an understanding of (and know the difference between) an income statement, a balance sheet, and a cash flow statement and that you understand the basic principles of accounting.

- Ensure that you have a comprehensive accounting package that provides relevant management reports and key indicators, accurately and timeously.

- Make sure that you have proper financial controls that are adhered to. Review them regularly to ensure that you have not introduced unnecessary rules or centralized controls. Watch out for controls that might encourage undesirable behavior inadvertently. In particular, ask whether any of your controls restrict design thinking.

- Develop an annual budget and monitor performance in line with it.

- Have your organization audited independently once a year.

- Speak to your accountant or tax advisor to determine how to reduce your effective tax rate.

9.3 Risk Management

AWARENESS

Business is about undertaking risk for reward. Risks are uncertain future events that, if not managed, could have a detrimental effect on your organization. Risk is an inherent part of running any organization. Maintaining the balance between risk and reward is part and parcel of everyday management.

There are several typical risks categories, including:

- Industry risks such as continually requiring capital investment, reducing margins, oversupply, business cycle volatility, and anything that might impact the industry as a whole.

- Technology risks, such as technology-enabled changes and processes becoming obsolete.

- Brand risks, including brand erosion.

- Competitor growth, such as changing competitive behavior, new competitors, or disruptive technologies.

- Customer changes, such as in customer behavior, changing customer needs, and relying on too few customers.

- Project risks, such as the failure of internal improvements, new business development, or a merger.

- Sales disruptions or stagnation.

- Disruption technologies that change the entire operating landscape.

- Other risks, such as financing, operational or hazardous risks.

Organizations will manage risk differently depending on their nature, their management, and the availability of resources.

There are four basic strategies to risk control:

- *Terminate* the activity that gives rise to the potential risk where there are no cost-effective mitigation strategies and where the cost of the risk outweighs any possible benefit.

- *Accept* the risk where no further effective or efficient controls are possible.

- *Reduce* the risk through appropriate controls.

- *Transfer* the risk through, for example, buying insurance.

ACTION

The following actions will help you to improve risk management:

- Identify broad areas of risk faced by the organization – for example, strategic risk, physical and operational risk, technology risk, credit risk, market risk, and compliance risk.

- Review the risks in terms of severity and likelihood:
  - Determine the severity of the risk on the organization, should it occur, as follows:
    - *Acceptable* = little or no impact
    - *Tolerable* = effects are felt but not critical to the outcome
    - *Undesirable* = serious impact on the desired outcome
    - *Intolerable* = could result in disaster
  - Determine the likelihood of the risk occurring:
    - *Improbable* = unlikely to occur

- o *Possible* = will most likely occur
- o *Probable* = will occur.
- Based on your severity and likelihood review, categorize the risks facing your organization:
  - o Low: The consequences of the risk are minor and unlikely to occur. Generally, ignore these risks.
  - o Medium: Somewhat likely to occur, these risks come with slightly more severe consequences. Not a priority area, but take action where necessary.
  - o High: These are serious risks that have significant consequences and are likely to occur. They need to be managed urgently in the short-term.
- Determine practical mitigation strategies to minimize the impact of the risk, should it occur. Focus on the *high* risks only. The *medium* and *low* risks can be ignored at this stage but should be reviewed periodically to determine whether their impact or likelihood has changed.
  - Have a disaster recovery plan.
  - Develop documentation and processes to keep a record of risks, mitigation strategies, and costs and losses owing to non-compliance.
  - Integrate risk-management plans into your strategic plans, where appropriate.
- Communicate risk-management policies to all employees.
- Once you have devised and implemented mitigation strategies, periodically review the success of these strategies in reducing the risk, with a particular focus on the *high* risks.
  - Review the severity of the risk in light of the mitigation strategies using the same scale as described above.

- Review the likelihood of the risk occurring using the same descriptors as above.

- Categorize the risk level based on the revised severity and likelihood rating using the same scale as above.

- For each risk, decide whether the result is acceptable or not.

10

Review your Target
Operating Model

Congratulations on defining how you intend to deliver your strategy through your Target Operating Model. Before continuing with implementation, review what you have done so far: (See *REVIEW YOUR TARGET OPERATING MODEL)*

- Do all the different elements of your target operating model work together? What do you need to change to improve integration?

- Take the areas of improvement you identified in each of the reviews you conducted of your current operations and convert them into projects. Keep these projects as simple as possible. *The section that follows provides an overview of project prioritization and project management.*

- Prioritize the projects you selected and identify those that are likely to have the most significant impact on achieving your vision within your limited resources.

- Make sure you have sufficient resources to implement each project successfully.

- Start implementing your priority projects.

- Keep track of your implementation. Consider using a project management application to help you keep track of all the projects you are implementing.

- Keep strategy execution top of mind for yourself and your management team, regardless of your daily work challenges.

- Communicate your vision and strategy to your employees so that they understand their role in achieving it. Identify and resolve areas of resistance.

You have completed reviewing your organization and have defined what you need to do to align it with your strategy. You are now ready for implementation.

Implementation is fraught with high levels of failure. Review the next section on implementation pitfalls and adjust your implementation plans accordingly.

REVIEW YOUR TARGET OPERATING MODEL

Review your target operating model by going through each of the sections below:

MARKETS, CUSTOMERS, AND REVENUE

Review how you intend to find, win, and retain customers. Is this sufficient to achieve the growth envisaged in your vision? Ask yourself:

- What area of specialization is achieved through your products and services?

- How do you differentiate yourself from your competitors? Why do customers buy from you? What is your unique selling proposition?

- How do you segment your customer base in terms of demographics and psychographics? Who are your best groupings of customers? What are your customers' needs within each segment? How do you meet these needs?

- Where do you focus your time, money, and resources in marketing your organization? Are these activities aligned to attaining your growth targets?

- How can you grow sales with your existing client base? Is this sufficient to meet your targets?

- How can you find and attract new customers to achieve your vision?

OPERATIONS

Meeting your customers' needs is achieved through delivery. Your value chain, resources, delivery partners, and structure are key to this delivery. Ask yourself what needs to change for you to attain your vision.

- Will your current operations deliver your vision?

- What support functions do you need to enable your organization to achieve its vision? Will these functions be outsourced or created in-house?

- Do you have the correct resources, are they sufficient, and are they optimally allocated to achieve our vision?

- Will your current delivery partners help you to achieve your vision?

- Is your resource allocation (as detailed in your budget) aligned to your delivery requirements?

- Will your current structure help or hinder attaining your vision?

EFFICIENCIES

How do you intend to improve efficiencies within your organization?

- What do you need to do to ensure that your employees are able to deliver the vision?

- What performance efficiencies have you identified, and what needs to happen to ensure that you deliver on these efficiencies?

- What information do you need to make timely decisions? How will you get this information?

CORPORATE GOVERNANCE

- Corporate governance is critical to any organization, particularly one that is growing.

- What changes are necessary to your governance structures to support your organization?

- Do you have appropriate financial (and other) controls and risk-management practices in place to ensure adequate governance?

SECTION 3:

IMPLEMENTATION

This is the third and final section outlined in the approach and is highlighted in the diagram below:

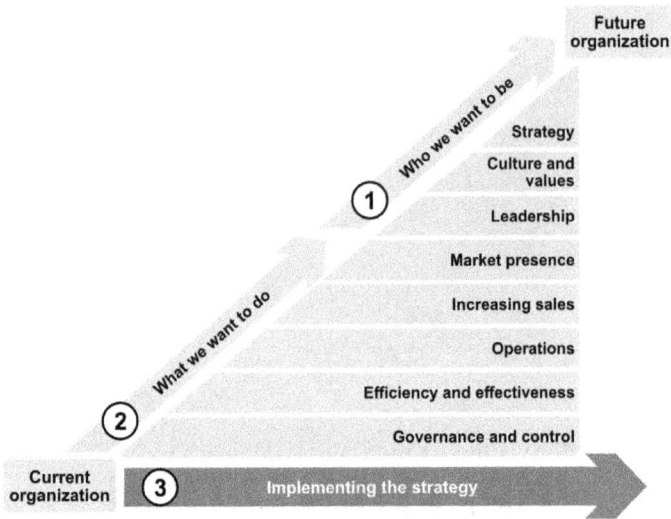

Section 3 of the Tool

Implementation is the key activity in getting your strategy to work for you. It is during the implementation phase that a large number of organizations fail. The purpose of this module is to outline the major pitfalls that organizations fail to plan for during implementation. It also provides a brief overview of project management as a tool for you to use when implementing your strategy.

11

Implementing Your Strategy

11.1 Implementation Tips

REASONS FOR FAILURE

Research has found that up to 75% of large organizations struggle to implement their strategies. The most common reasons for this are:

- **Inadequate or Insufficient Allocation of Resources**
  Resource allocation is key to implementing the strategy. Organizations often introduce a new strategy that should have far-reaching impacts on the allocation of resources, yet they fail to reallocate those same resources. This is

exacerbated where they are insufficient resources available to deliver the strategy.

- **Insufficient or Unclear Communication of the Organization's Vision and Strategy**
  The majority of workforces throughout the world do not know (or understand) the strategies employed by their organizations. They are unaware of how they contribute to their organization's success and, in particular, of their impact on achieving any vision or strategy. It is vital to have ongoing and frequent communication of the vision and strategy – and of the role each member of the team has in achieving the vision.

- **Leadership not Placing Enough Emphasis on Achieving the Vision and Strategy**
  Many leadership teams get caught up in daily work challenges rather than in leading the organization into the future. Too little time is spent on selling the vision and monitoring the implementation of the strategies. This is compounded by actions and decisions that are fragmented and not aligned to the vision, ambiguous or conflicting goals and responsibilities, no clear priorities, silo behavior, and turf protection.

- **Rewards Systems not Linked to Achieving Strategies**
  Strategies are changed, but reward systems (particularly for managers) are focused on achieving old objectives. Behavior thus stays the same, and strategies are not implemented.

- **Performance Indicators not Linked to the New Strategies**
  The organization has a new strategy but the performance indicators are still measuring performance against the old strategy, or don't measure key aspects of the new strategy.

- **Over-Complexity of Solutions Required to Deliver the Strategy**
  Initiatives can sometimes be too complex for the organization's resources and capabilities. This can be made worse by delays in developing solutions, a lack of plans, or inadequate project management.

- **Resistance to Change**
  Either the organization's culture drives the resistance, or the organization is ineffective in driving the required change. This is made worse where leadership and management pay lip service to, but don't support, the change.

- **Strategies not Adapting to Changing Internal or External Circumstances**
  The marketplace is in continuous change. Your strategies need to be flexible enough to change as circumstances change.

STEPS TO IMPROVE STRATEGY IMPLEMENTATION

The entire tool has been designed to identify and define strategies to improve performance, with the end objective of achieving your vision. Some of the key initiatives to ensure that your strategy is implemented are discussed below.

While going through the tool, you would have identified a number of implementation projects and tasks for your organization. Start by reviewing these in light of the failure factors listed above. What can you do to improve your chances of strategy implementation success? The list is not exhaustive, so do not be limited in your thinking.

The sections below takes each of the challenges listed above and suggests an approach to mitigate the risk of failure in each area. You might need to revisit each area to check that you are reducing the risk of implementation failure.

Resource allocation

Resource allocation is key to getting your strategy implemented. Review the resources that are needed to implement the strategy and then reallocate resources where necessary. Should employees be shifted around in the organization? Do teams need restructuring? What support will your employees need as they are moved to new positions? Do you need additional skills? Will your assets meet your future needs? Will your strategic partners meet the needs of your strategy? Will you need to change your operating model? Will your structure meet your future needs?

One key element is your budget. Is your budget a repeat of last year, or have you reworked it completely to be aligned with your strategy?

Once you have determined your resource needs, you might find you have insufficient funding. Strategy is often a set of choices and trade-offs regarding where you will invest, compete and win. Failure to make decisions on trade-offs could compromise your entire strategy. Review all your strategies and allocate resources to the most important functions, and mothball other initiatives for the future.

Revisit the **Operations** *module for more information on resource allocation.*

Vision and strategy communication

You need to communicate your vision and strategies with all employees at every level. This is not a once-off but a regular communication event providing feedback on progress in achieving the vision. Make a point of engaging with your employees regularly – in an informal way – on their role, asking for feedback on their views. You want each employee not only to understand where you are taking the organization but also the part they are to play in getting it there. Employees are more motivated to achieve the vision if they understand the big picture and their role in it.

*Revisit the **Strategy** module for ideas on how to communicate your strategy.*

Time spent on leading strategy implementation

How regularly do you and your leadership team discuss progress in achieving your strategy? Many organizations spend less than an hour a month. This is insufficient time if you are serious about achieving your vision. Make your strategy a fixed agenda item for all your management meetings. Discussion should not only be centered on progress in achieving your vision but also on discussing external developments that might impact your organization.

Strategy should not be an annual planning exercise but rather an ongoing exercise in improving your organization's performance both now and into the future.

*Revisit the **Leadership and Delegation** module for more information on this topic.*

Reward system

What kind of performance does your reward system encourage? Is there a balance between (short-term) performance and attaining your (long-term) strategy? Who is accountable for implementing each step in the strategic plan? What are the consequences of not implementing the strategy?

*Revisit the section on **Rewards** in the **Your Employees as Partners** module for more information.*

Performance measurement

How do you know when your organization is achieving its strategy? Develop effective measures that measure not only ongoing performance but also the attainment of your strategic goals. Make sure these are effective and are measured regularly. Ensure that you measure strategy attainment frequently enough that you can take timely corrective action where necessary.

*Revisit the **Measuring Your Performance** module for more information on this topic*

Project management

Project management is a critical practice when implementing more complex changes to your organization. Where possible, define your interventions as projects, and then manage them accordingly, using standard project management practices and a project management tool or app.

*The next module provides an overview of **Project Management**.*

Solution complexity

Complex strategies and solutions have a higher rate of failure!

How complex are your strategic initiatives in design and implementation? Is there a simpler way to achieve the same objective? Does your organization have a history of implementing complex initiatives successfully? Can your organization handle the complexity of your strategy?

Aim at keeping all aspects of your strategy and its attainment simple. You will have a greater chance of success.

Resistance to change

There are two elements to resistance to change.

The first is: How good are you at change? Can your organization respond quickly to a changing external environment? This could be from political or regulatory changes, disruptive technologies, natural disasters, or pandemics.

The second is about your employees and their resistance to the changes necessary to implement the strategies. A key aspect to the successful implementation of any initiative is change management. You need to have a defined program on how you will introduce change to your employees so that they will support the change.

Revisit the **Renewing Your Organization** *module of this book for additional information.*

CONCLUSION

Your strategy does not end with an annual strategic planning session. If you want to implement your strategy successfully, you need to work at it and at its implementation.

This module has highlighted the most common reasons for strategy implementation failure. There might be other factors that are not addressed here that could impact your strategy's successful implementation. Go through your strategy and see where you can improve things to increase your likelihood of success.

11.2 Project Management

Project management is a useful tool to help you keep track of the actions you want to implement for the changes you want to introduce.

Project management is a process of defining and planning an intervention, putting these plans into action, and monitoring their performance. It is an inherently complex process. This module, loosely based on the *Berenschot Project Management Model*[28], aims to simplify the project management process.

PROJECT LIFE CYCLE

There are four generic stages to a project, as depicted in the diagram below: *Definition, Design, Execution,* and *After-care.*

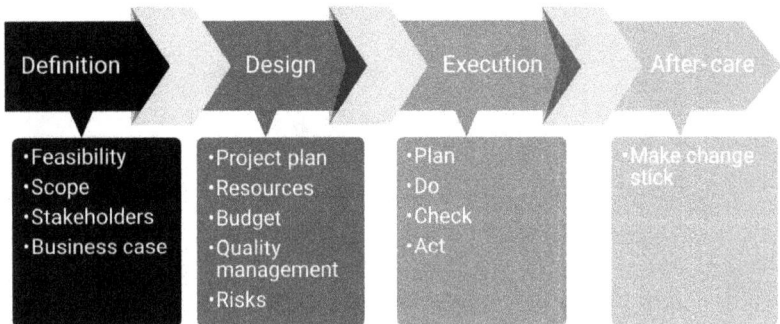

Definition	Design	Execution	After-care
•Feasibility •Scope •Stakeholders •Business case	•Project plan •Resources •Budget •Quality management •Risks	•Plan •Do •Check •Act	•Make change stick

Berenschot Project Management Model

---

28   Mikael Krogerus and Roman Tschäppeler, The Decision Book: Fifty Models for Strategic Thinking, Profile Books, 2017.

The four project stages are discussed in detail below.

Definition

- **Determine the feasibility of the project in solving the problem identified**

Fully define the problem you are trying to solve. Determine the solution you envisage to address the problem. Determine whether the solution solves the problem.

- **Define the project purpose or project scope**

What are you trying to achieve? What are the project deliverables? What benefits will derive from the project? What are the objectives and goals of the project? What is included in the project, and what is not included? How will project success be measured?

- **Determine which of your organization's stakeholders will be impacted by (or may impact) the project**

These could be your employees or external stakeholders, like customers, suppliers, and funders. Have a change management plan in place detailing how you will manage the impact of stakeholders on the project. Your change management plan is a critical component of getting your project implemented.

- **Determine a project business case**

The project business case will allow you to explore the benefits of the project against its anticipated costs.

Design

- Once you have defined what you want from the project, you can define how you want to go about delivering it. This becomes the **project plan** and includes actions or tasks, responsibilities, and timelines:

- All projects with some degree of complexity will consist of several sub-projects. A useful starting point is to define these sub-projects and to understand the relationships between them fully.

- Break each sub-project into tasks. It is useful for each task to have a specific, measurable outcome or deliverable.

- Determine whether any task is dependent on the completion of any other task.

- Once the tasks are defined, allocate start and end dates for the completion of each. Review your tasks and timelines, making sure that they are achievable and that the order of tasks makes practical sense.

- Decide who is going to be responsible for the delivery of each task.

- Capture your plans into a project management tool.

- Review your project scope while planning and determining the **resources** required to deliver the project. Who will deliver the project? Will they deliver the project in addition to doing their regular jobs? Will you need additional people? What other resources (equipment, facilities, hardware, and software) do you need to complete the project?

- Knowing what resources are required will help you to define a **project budget**. You can review the project budget against the benefits you expect from the project and then decide whether to go ahead with the project or not.

- The **quality** of project output is always a challenge. It is critical that you know how you are going to ensure a quality end deliverable.

- All projects potentially face **risks** that can impact their outcome negatively. Undertake a project risk analysis and determine how you are going to mitigate the identified risks.

- Document your plans in a **project charter**, which will serve as a reference point as the project progresses. A project charter is a short, written document (ideally a one-pager) that defines the key points from your deliberations during your project definition. It consists of the project scope, the project plan, the project budget (including required resources – people and other), the quality management approach, the project risks and mitigation strategies, and the project stakeholder management and communications plan.

- Get your project team together and launch the project. Once you have appointed your project team, make sure they fully understand the project. Ask them to report back to you their understanding of what they are trying to achieve and how they plan to deliver the project. Ensure that your team has sufficient skills and resources to deliver the project successfully and that they will not be overworked.

- If you have too many projects on the go and need to prioritize, refer to the *PROJECT PORTFOLIO MATRIX* box at the end of this module.

Execution

There are four repetitive steps to managing any project – *Plan, Do, Check,* and *Act.*

Project Execution Steps

To ensure that the project is going to deliver what you envisaged, on time, and within budget, set aside time to have regular report-back meetings with your team to discuss and review:

- Their progress against the project objectives, plans, and budget.
- Their outputs and the quality thereof.
- Stakeholder management and communication progress.
- Any project roadblocks and risks (and possible solutions).
- Expenditure against the project budget.

Celebrate key milestones with the team and recognize their contribution to the success of the project.

Aftercare

Many projects fail post-implementation. It is easy for people to slip back into old ways of doing things rather than changing how they do them. Not all interventions are going to work as planned. It is essential to monitor the implementation of the intervention continually and to take appropriate action.

PROJECT PORTFOLIO MATRIX

Got too much on your hands? Juggling one too many projects, both professionally and personally? Not sure which projects to focus on or which to drop?

The Project Portfolio Matrix is a flexible tool that will help you to decide which projects to pursue.

1. Start by defining *two* criteria or parameters with which

to access the projects you currently have underway. Such criteria could include:

    a. Costs (including financial, resources, and stress) versus time (including time to completion and time to reward).

    b. Achievement of personal objectives versus how much you are learning.

    c. The benefit to the organization versus the costs.

2. Determine how you will score projects against the criteria. In our example below, we use *cost versus time*. You might measure time as *behind*, *on time*, or *ahead of schedule*. Costs might be measured as *underspent*, *on budget*, or *overspent*.

3. Take these criteria and draw up a Project Portfolio Matrix similar to the one in the diagram below.

4. List each project in which you are involved and score it from a stakeholder perspective or from your perspective.

5. Score each project against the criteria, and plot them on the matrix, as follows:

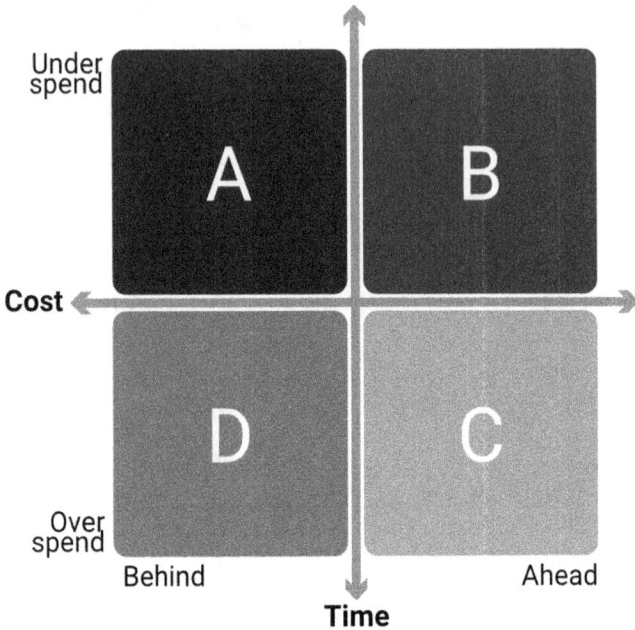

Project Portfolio Matrix

6. Interpret the results based on the criteria you chose. In the *cost versus time* example, you could evaluate the results as follows:

- **Underspend/Behind:** Why are you underspending? Will increasing expenditure improve delivery? What remedial action do you need to take?

- **Underspend/Ahead:** The ideal situation. Continue with these projects. What can you learn from these projects to apply to other projects?

- **Overspend/Ahead:** Are you ahead because of an overspend? What is the projected situation? Do you need to take remedial action?

- **Overspend/Behind:** The worst scenario! Should you be closing the project down? What remedial action should you take?

Adapted from Mikael Krogerus and Roman Tschäppelar's *The Decision Book – Fifty Models for Strategic Thinking.*

A Final Word

Congratulations! You have completed the tool. By now, you should be well on your way to implementing your strategy successfully.

The tool has been designed as both a strategy definition and implementation tool and a business improvement tool. You can use it on an ongoing basis as new business challenges come your way. By improving continuously, you become a learning organization. By repeating the modules, you will come up with many new ideas that you might not have considered during your first review. You will certainly find the whole process much easier the second time around.

I wish you well in your endeavors to implement your strategy and improve your organization's performance.

Should you have any questions, success stories, or suggestions on how to improve the tool, I would love to hear from you. Please feel free to get in touch with me through my publisher at tom@simplifytom.com.

Acknowledgments

To every author who has taken the time to share their management theories through books and academic articles, thank you. Whether these theories take off and become popular practices or not, we can learn from them and find possible solutions to our organization's challenges. These authors add to our pool of knowledge continually, and without them, this tool would probably never have been written.

A special word of thanks goes out to the many people who have added to the richness of this tool. In particular, I would like to acknowledge the inputs of John Shorten, Dr. George Lucas, Jane McGreggor, Mike Melvill, Dr. Hilton Vergotine, and Dave Wilson. Their reviews and critical inputs greatly improved the content and how it was presented in this book.

My editor, Phillipa Mitchell, has been fantastic in improving the readability of the book through pointing out logic errors, inconsistencies, English language usage improvements, and other editing issues. Phillipa has also held my hand through this my first venture into indie publishing. Ricky Woods did a great job in giving a final polish to the words of the book. Gregg Davies has been fantastic in improving the illustrations and in creating the book's look and feel. Thanks to a great production team.

Finally, to my wife and family, thank you for supporting me through the many challenges I experienced while writing and completing this book. Your encouragement and belief in me kept me going. Without you, I would not have reached the finish line.

About the Author

Mike Shorten has more than thirty-five years of formal consulting experience across various industries, including research and development, agriculture, wholesale and distribution, services, training, mining, manufacturing, tourism, electricity generation, and the public sector. He has led multiple projects focusing on strategy development and execution, target operating model definition, business process engineering and enterprise project management. He has worked with businesses across the size spectrum, from SMMEs to large listed corporations and government entities.

Mike has worked for international consultancies and has a realistic view of where value can and cannot be added to a client's business. Complex solutions often end in failure. His business philosophy is to simplify.

His primary strengths are in helping organizations define and implement strategies. This entails identifying problems or opportunities, facilitating strategy definition, defining operating models, determining actions to implement strategies, and in the implementation thereof. His passion lies in defining solutions to problems and then turning these solutions into methodologies.

Mike lives in Johannesburg, South Africa, with his wife, son and daughter, and much-loved staffie. Mike has a love for the African bush and dreams of a second career working in a game reserve.

www.ingramcontent.com/pod-product-compliance
Lightning Source LLC
Chambersburg PA
CBHW071328210326
41597CB00015B/1379